GCSE Home Economics

FAMILIES AND CHILD DEVELOPMENT

Sharon Goodyer

Longman

The books in this series

Food for Health by Dodie Roe
Home and Consumer by Dodie Roe
Textiles for People by Maureen Wilkinson
Dodie Roe is also Series editor.

The following topics relevant to this book are covered in other titles in the series.

Food for Health
Food for children.
Additives in food.

Home and Consumer
Children's rights.
Care labelling.
Environmental health and home safety.
Accidents in the home; home safety.
Advertising and labelling goods.

Textiles for People
Making fabric articles for children.
Children's clothes: suitability, labelling, and care.

Longman Group UK Limited
Longman House, Burnt Mill, Harlow,
Essex CM20 2JE, England
and Associated Companies throughout the world.

© Longman Group UK Limited 1988
All rights reserved; no part of this publication
may be reproduced, stored in a retrieval system,
or transmitted in any form or by any form or by means, electronic,
mechanical, photocopying, recording, or otherwise,
without the prior written permission of the Publishers.

First published 1988

Set in 10/12 point Palatino and Univers

Printed in Great Britain
by Hazell Watson & Viney Limited, Aylesbury

ISBN 0 582 22478 0

CONTENTS

ABC   1
– suggestions on how to use this book, why this is an important area for everyone to study, and help in making good decisions.

Babies   12
– the place of babies in our society and how families can cope with and enjoy their babies.

Books and television   20
– how to make the best use of these with children.

Celebrations   27
– different ways of enjoying a wide variety of happy occasions.

Childcarers   34
– a look at several ways of helping families to provide the sort of care young children need.

Children have rights   42
– a worldwide view of how children are treated.

Clothes   47
– likes and dislikes and good value for money.

Disability and handicap   54
– the causes of disability, our attitudes, and ways of being constructive.

Diseases and immunisation   66
– how immunisation works and the situation in Great Britain and in other countries.

Experts   72
– how best to use expert advice.

Facts of life   78
– important information about growing up and a look at the ways in which we gain our knowledge about sex.

Families   90
– an up-to-date picture of today's families and a look at different ways of becoming a family member.

Feelings and behaviour   100
– imagine what it feels like to be a child and try to understand why they behave as they do.

Feet and shoes 109
– decisions about feet and shoes are often difficult and expensive, and it is not easy to correct mistakes later.

Food and drink 116
– why do many babies and children eat so badly?

Health and illness 125
– the promotion of good health and coping with minor illness.

Home and going out 131
– home is important to all of us but it is also the place where most accidents happen.

Playing 142
– remember what it feels like to play, and find out how to provide good play opportunities for children.

Talking 152
– enjoying language and getting better at using it.

Toys 159
– household objects as toys, generations of children have enjoyed the same sorts of toys, and how to cope with today's advertising.

XYZ 169
– producing your most interesting work for assessment, using what you have learned in the future, and how to continue learning.

Addresses 174
– useful sources of information.

Index 181
– an alphabetical list of key words and phrases to help you use this book.

Preface

This book is one of a series of four, written particularly to help teachers interpret and pupils succeed in the GCSE examination courses in Home Economics. The authors have worked together on developing a problem-solving approach and have tried out ideas in the classroom. The other books in the series are:

Home and Consumer
Textiles for People
Food for Health

What is so special about this examination?
One of the aims of the GCSE examination course is to develop the skills of decision making, which are necessary throughout life. It also aims to help individuals to lead effective lives as members of the family and community, and to provide them with the management skills to use resources wisely and to recognise the interrelationship between the need for food, clothing, shelter, and security.

What does this approach entail?
The authors of these books have used the subject matter of Home Economics to provide pupils with opportunities to:
- identify needs in a particular area;
- recall, seek out, and apply knowledge relevant to the situation;
- identify ways of carrying out a task or solving a problem, isolating the priorities;
- decide upon and plan a course of action;
- carry out a course of action;
- evaluate the effectiveness of the course of action.

It is hoped that if pupils are able to develop decision making skills they will be able to recall and apply these criteria in different situations.

How do these books help with this approach?
The books are written with an alphabetical sequence of topics, similar to a catalogue, not as a course to be followed through from beginning to end. Units of work from within one book, or from across several, can therefore be put together as the teacher wishes. This supports the underlying philosophy of the GCSE course to integrate the four main aspects of Home Economics.

The topics in the catalogue start from the pupils' own knowledge, provide trigger material, practical exercises, discussion points, ideas for visits and speakers, and suggest resources which might be used to extend experience.

Families and Child Development is about issues which are sometimes considered personal and sensitive. This book starts from the pupils' present lives and lets the pupils investigate these issues in a careful way. While doing this they are encouraged to develop skills such as information-seeking, and also to come to realise that there is rarely a perfect decision but that it is worthwhile exercising care, thought, and effort in trying to reach a best possible solution.

Dodie Roe
Series editor

About using this book

There are two very special things about this book:

You will be learning about yourself now as well as learning about families and children for the future.

There will be opportunities for **you** to practise making decisions.

Nobody can survive without making decisions. Even when we think we have avoided making a decision our actions often prove otherwise and to put off making a decision is a decision in itself!

In this first Topic you will see that **your** decisions are important straight away, and throughout this book you will be encouraged to seek out information, particularly from your district Health Education/Promotion Unit. (This is a government-funded body whose main purpose is to keep the public informed about important matters related to health.) The information you need to make good decisions does change because we find out more all the time; so it is very important to become skilful at obtaining, understanding, and using information for the future. We can all get better at making decisions, but there is no perfect decision in any situation. What is right for one person is not necessarily right for another. What seems right for today might not look so good tomorrow. It is therefore important not only to learn to be tolerant of other people's decisions but also to have the strength and ability to make one's own.

Decisions in this area of life are sometimes the most important and controversial we will ever make in our lives. They often have the most serious consequences for ourselves and for others. This book aims to give you a chance to preview the processes involved in making these decisions, to "try out" some of the possible routes, and to come as close as possible to feeling and experiencing the consequences.

In surveys conducted amongst adults it was found that one of the greatest sources of stress and unhappiness is an inability to cope with the sorts of situations described in this book.

Each Topic starts with a section to help you to prepare yourself. Throughout each Topic there are activities for you to do. At the end there are exercises to try. These will help you to see the Topic material in context and to practise using what you have learned. Finally, there are suggestions for other relevant Topics in this book, or in this series of books, and also ideas for other things for you to do, like places to visit, or people you could invite to come to school.

You will almost certainly find that you know a great deal about these important Topics already so be sure to share your experiences and enjoy listening to other people's. Remember you do not have to have children of your own or even plan to have them to be involved in making decisions about children. This is the point at which the first Topic in this book starts.

There are three symbols used in this book:

means that you have to "collect" something.

means that you have to "send for" something.

means that you can find out more information by looking either in another part of this book; or in another book in this series; or in a computer program, leaflet, booklet, or other publication; or by visiting somewhere or asking someone to visit you.

Author's acknowledgement
I would like to thank all the children, parents, teachers, and playgroup leaders who have taught me over the past few years.

Dedication
This book is dedicated to my family and especially to Nick, Catherine, and Richard.

Illustrations by Chris Ryley

ABC

Collect ideas, pictures, and articles about adults' responsibilities to children (such as protecting them from danger or providing them with suitable food).
Send for leaflets such as "Your Children Need You" from your district Health Education/Promotion Unit (address on page 174). "Your Children Need You" helps to explain in how many different ways adults, and particularly parents, are important to young children.

Getting started

Before you start using this book stop and think what you expect to gain from it. Have a quick look at the Contents pages, flip through the book, and then look at one or two topics more carefully. Now that you know what sort of things are in this book ask yourself a few questions such as "Are these important things to learn about?", "When am I going to need to be able to do these things?", "When might this information be useful?", and "What do I know and feel about these issues already?" You should also use the Index to help you to find things you are particularly interested in.

Anybody can look after young children. It is a natural thing to do. You don't need any special training.

What do you think? Can you give any evidence to back up your point of view?

This book will give you plenty of opportunities to learn about families, and it will help you to practise making decisions about children. You will find out how children develop, and you will learn how to respond to them in a caring, sensible way.

What are your attitudes **now** towards some of the Topics in this book? Complete the following sentences to help you to get your thoughts organised:

Imagine you are a parent with a young child. Living with me are . . . My young child has changed my life in these ways . . . As a parent I go out to work because . . . As a parent I do not go out to work because . . . Some things which cause a problem for me as a parent are . . . Some things about having my child which give me happiness are . . . I think I am a good parent because . . . If I were a bad parent I would . . .

Look at each other's replies and give each point mentioned the correct letter according to the chart below. Go as far down the chart as possible each time.

A	Irrelevant
B	Relevant
C	To do with needs of child and parent
D	To do with needs of parent only
E	To do with needs of child only
F	To do with physical needs of child
G	To do with psychological needs of child

You will probably find it quite difficult to decide what letter to give some of the points, but discuss this amongst yourselves and then make the best decision you can. Count up how many of each letter you have. What sort of things have you learned about your and your friends' attitudes?

I need to know about this

You will find using this book especially interesting if you try to make sure that you have a good reason for studying a particular Topic. "Childcarers", "Talking", "Children have rights", or "Disability and handicap" could be useful to you straight away in everyday situations, like those in figure 1.

This book is a good starting point for you. Send for the free leaflets suggested at the start of each Topic. Discuss what you are learning about with all sorts of different people. Carry out your own investigations. Start to sort out what your feelings and opinions are. This will all make your work more interesting and it will help you to make better decisions.

Your decisions are important

We are all responsible for the young children around us, in our community. Every day we make decisions that affect their lives.

Figure 1 Everyday situations.

Figure 2 Your decisions affect others.

How have the decisions in figure 2 affected children? Are they important? Can you think of any other decisions people take every day which affect children?

Some people are trained to help them make good decisions about children. How many jobs can you think of where this sort of training would be necessary?

Because lots of everyday decisions taken by untrained people affect children, some people think there should be a government Minister for Children. This Minister would try to stop people taking decisions which harmed children and would make sure that the rights of children were upheld.

Other people think it would be better if we were all helped, with information and training, to make better decisions.

In pairs suggest three things you think the Minister should do, *or* design a handout giving the public some suggestions as to what they need to know about young children. Use the information you received from your district Health Education/Promotion Unit and the articles you collected to help you do this.

Learning how to be a good parent

We learn about parenthood from our own childhood first. Then we might see how other parents behave when we visit another family. Later on we might go to National Childbirth Trust classes for support during the very early stages of being parents ourselves, and we will watch other parents with their young children. Most of us will become parents and there are many different ways of behaving as a parent. This is often a sensitive and sometimes a difficult thing to explore because new information and opinions might go against our own past experiences.

If you find this to be true remember that it is often possible to hold a different opinion from someone else and yet still understand their point of view. It is also possible for a number of different views to be right in some way or other.

Here are five reasons for learning about parenthood today:

1) By the age of sixteen one in five children will have divorced parents. This is upsetting and stressful for the children so the adults involved need to be especially thoughtful and caring.

2) Many children are treated badly by their parents. This can be because their own parents did not show them how to be good parents.

3) There is new evidence to show that the good health of the man and the woman before they start a family is important to the health of the baby. There is still research going on, and this will result in more important new information.

4) The effects of unemployment give parents new difficulties to cope with. These can be social and emotional as well as financial.

5) There were 74,800 children in care in this country in 1984. This shows how much help families still need.

As you can see there is still a great deal that needs to be done to provide better care for the next generation of children. Some of these things are to do with changes which could be made by government and laws, by the Health Service, in standards of living, and by group action; but they are also to do with **decisions made by you**.

What can I do to make my decisions better?

DDD **D**efine clearly what it is you want.

E E E **E**xplain the problem clearly.

C C C **C**ollect the information and sort it out.

I I I **I**nvestigate your choices.

S S S **S**ort out what other people think.

I I I **I**magine what effect each of your choices might have.

OOO **O**pt for one of your choices and carry it out.

NNN **N**ote what happens and think whether you are satisfied.

S S S **S**tart again if changes are needed.

The side of this page is shaded in grey so that you can find it again easily. You will need it when you start making the decisions.

Your beliefs about what is right or wrong will have a lot of influence on the decisions you make. However, it is always possible to change your mind about what you think is the right way to behave. In fact this would sometimes be a very sensible thing to do as circumstances change and you learn more about situations, hear other people's points of view, and understand the consequences of actions more thoroughly.

Here is an example of one thing which most of us will have changed our minds about as we grew up: adults accept fantasy stories from very young children but teach older ones that they must always try to tell the truth, and then later on the children begin to understand that perhaps in certain situations a "white lie" might be right.

Now try these

Describe two decisions which you or your friends have made which might have affected young children. How could you have changed your decisions for the better? If you find it difficult to remember real decisions "make up" two situations and suggest how the people might have acted.

What sort of things do you think a food shop manager/ess, an architect, a bus driver, a mobile ice-cream seller, and a police man/woman should know about children?

Can you imagine how the following experiences might cause us to change our opinions about what is right or wrong? What might these people's opinions have been before and after these events?

A fourth year pupil regularly visits some Down's syndrome children at their special school. (To find out more about this handicap refer to the Topic *Disability and Handicap*.)
A 17-year-old unmarried girl discovers that she is pregnant.
A 25-year-old married man finds out he is infertile and unable to become a father.
A second year pupil learns the facts about the real risks of smoking.
A fifth year pupil falls in love with a pupil from a different ethnic background and religion.

Figure 3 shows an example of a poor decision with regard to young children.
　Look at the page with the shaded edge and suggest which parts of the decision-making process could have been improved to produce a better decision. What do you think might have caused the planners to build only flights of steps?

Figure 3 An example of poor planning.

Can you find any examples of bad planning with regard to young children in the area where you live? Adults who are responsible for children might be able to "open your eyes" to difficulties you have not noticed.

People who manage shops have to make a lot of difficult decisions which directly affect the public.

Where do you think you would put the children's shoes if you managed the shop in figure 4?

We don't sell many children's shoes so we put them upstairs.

I can't drag the children up those stairs. What do I do with the buggy?

If I can't see the shoes I want at the front of the shop I don't go in.

Figure 4 *A difficult decision.*

How many different opinions about the decision in figure 5 can you find by asking around? Try to group these opinions. You could put together all the ones you agree with. Can you suggest two other ways of grouping them?

Figure 5 Parents make most decisions about children.

Our attitudes affect our decisions, so what do you think are the *worst* things to do? Judge the acts or situations below in terms of "wrongness" by writing them on separate sheets of paper and then ranking them in order of "wrongness". Put the worst act at the bottom of your pile of pieces of paper. When you have finished compare your order with one other person and, through discussion, come to one order you can agree on. Now compare your order with another pair's.

Going out with your best friend's girl or boyfriend without telling them.
Having affairs whilst married.
Seeking a divorce when you both agree on it.
A 15-year-old girl taking the contraceptive pill to prevent conception.
Not marrying the person you love because your family advise against it.
Doctors not doing absolutely everything within their power to keep alive a handicapped baby.
A mother leaving home and the young children staying in their father's care.
Keeping quiet when you suspect someone of mistreating a child.

Choose a real-life situation from the list below and work through the decision-making process carefully. Keep a record of your ideas, notes, and work. Carry out your decision. What do you think about your results? How could you do better next time? In each situation there are suggestions for where you might look for help in collecting information.

1) You are trying to find or make several as near as possible sugar-free drinks young children will like because a friend has told you how worried she is about the amount of sugar her children have in their cold and hot drinks. Recipe books, ingredients' labels, and a home economics teacher might be able to help.

2) Five-year-olds often have trouble doing up the laces on their shoes, tying knots in their ties, making bows, and doing threading or simple sewing. Can you make several attractive but economical toys or activities which will encourage them to practise these skills? Looking in toy shops or catalogues which sell toys and talking to a nursery school teacher might help.

3) A 3-year-old wants to learn how to use scissors. Can you help her learn? Can you think of a simple but effective picture she could make as soon as she can use scissors? An art teacher or a playgroup leader might be able to help.

4) You know that there is something worrying your friend. Your friend has tried to tell you what it is but just can't find the words. Can you think of any ways to help your friend? What sort of words and actions are best for you to use in this situation? Somebody who is used to helping others in this way such as a Youth Club leader or a counsellor inside a school might be a help, or you could try talking to friends to find out what has helped them when discussing sensitive matters. The nearest you will probably be able to come to

carrying out your decision(s) is to ask a friend to rôle play having a problem. You could then ask them how they felt about the way you tackled the situation.

5) What sort of a holiday would you recommend for a family with young children? Write a list of eight important points to consider when choosing such a holiday. Then, using some brochures, prepare a chart which shows how three holidays compare with each other. Families with young children will be able to help you by telling you about their real-life experiences, and you and your friends will have memories of your own which will help when doing this work.

SEE ALSO

Experts to find out more about those people who try to help families with young children.
Families for more information about the many different types of families.

In your reference library there will be the British Humanities Index. If you look up subjects such as "Children" or "Family" there will be information which will help you to find interesting articles in magazines and newspapers which will also be in the library.

There is a computer program called "Quest". This could help you organise a large amount of information that you might have collected as a class, about a Topic.

Careers teachers help people to make decisions in one area of their lives. You could ask a careers teacher to come and talk to you about making important decisions.

Babies

Collect some pictures of babies in lots of different situations from magazines. For a week keep a record of all the situations where you see babies such as:

"On Sunday I saw a baby in a pram at the park. On Monday I saw a dad carrying his baby while I was waiting at the bus stop, and a mum and baby got on the bus on the way home."
Alternatively, you could list all the situations on television in which you see babies during one week.

Collect some towelling and some disposable nappies and a babywear catalogue. Send for information about giving birth and caring for babies; from your district Health Education/Promotion Unit (address on page 174).

Write to Birthright and the National Childbirth Trust (addresses pages 175 and 178), for leaflets about birth and babies.

Babies in public

To find out what sort of a public image babies have look carefully at all the pictures you have collected. Can you now say what image of a baby we are being offered? Do you think this is a true picture or not? Which sorts of behaviour and what kinds of appearance are over-emphasised? Are the babies mainly from one group in society? Was anything left out when these baby pictures were chosen?

Very few people nowadays come from large families where they have a lot of contact with and responsibility for babies. Most of us get our information about babies from our own past, from what we see in the media, from any courses we choose to study, and also from the babies we see as we lead our normal lives.

Compare your record of where you have seen babies recently with a list made by a friend. What sort of situations did you see?

Now make a chart showing how often you and other people in your group saw activities such as: bathtime, breastfeeding, crying, smiling, sleeping, nappy changing, waking up, adult cuddling and talking to a baby, and a baby in a pram. What other activities could you include in your chart? What does this chart tell you about your own everyday experience of babies?

How do you think the pictures of babies in places like knitting pattern covers and disposable nappy adverts affect a new parent's expectations of their baby? How might this affect their feelings and behaviour towards the baby?

Where babies are born

Read the Health Education/Promotion Unit's information, which will explain the choices parents can make about where their baby will be born. Which hospitals in your area have maternity units? Have you or any of your friends ever visited a mother in hospital with her new baby?

Perhaps you could interview one or two parents who have had babies recently and ask them to tell you about their experiences. What sort of questions do you want to ask? Try to record these interviews and then listen to them very carefully later. Are there any things that seem especially important to these parents?

It is important to check that babies are healthy as soon as they are born so that help can be given at once if necessary. It is also important that during the first few minutes of a baby's life there is as little medical interference as possible. The parents need time to get to know and begin to love and care for this new person. So the midwife uses a scorecard to check five simple things about a baby. The midwife checks that the baby looks healthy, that the baby cries strongly, that the baby's muscles are active, that the baby responds to being tickled on the foot, and that the baby's heart is beating steadily. All this can be done quickly and easily while the mother holds the baby and if the baby has a low "score" help can then be given.

Figure 6 Look what we can do!

Figure 7 I have feelings too.

Everybody always asks what the weight of a new baby is. This is a good sign of the baby's health and very low birth-weight babies need special care. This does not mean that the heavier babies are always healthier though. The average birth weight in this country is roughly seven pounds (3.2 kg).

The birth of every baby should be registered within forty-two days by a parent. This is free and is done by the local registrar of births, marriages, and deaths. The registrar will give the parent the official birth certificate and also the new child's NHS medical card.

How can you tell whether a baby is happy or not? What sort of feelings do happy and unhappy babies give you? How would you try to make the unhappy baby in figure 7 more content? Would it make *you* feel more happy to do this? If you were unable to stop the baby crying what would you feel like then? Remember babies do not know how they are making you feel. They are not doing it on purpose. How do you think you would feel trying to do something while you can hear a baby crying? You could ask a parent to record a baby crying and try to do your next lesson with this tape recording on!

Time to care?

Babies needs simple things like food, warmth, comfort, protection, and to be kept reasonably clean. They also need these things immediately. They are not being unreasonable–they simply have no way of understanding that something will happen in the future, even in a minute's time. These urgent needs can cause parents difficulties.

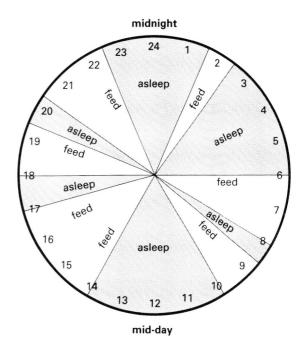

Figure 9 A baby's timetable.

Figure 8 A difficult situation.

What do you think the adult and the baby in figure 8 are feeling? Can you suggest two things the adult could do and explain the possible results of each?

What sort of difficulties might the 4-week-old baby's patterns of sleeping and feeding shown in figure 9 give the rest of the family? How might the family (and others) make the day easier? How many hours would the average family spend on various baby tasks every week? Use the evidence in figure 10 (over the page) to help you.

The evidence in figure 10 came from fifty-five families with small children. There were great differences between these families and the numbers given are averages. Each family was asked how long anyone in the household spent on basic child-care tasks. Seven-eighths of this time was given by the mother. There is evidence to show that fathers may be more involved in other aspects of their children's care. There was little regular help from relatives and friends. Two-thirds of the mothers said they did not have any spells of one hour or more in the week when they were free of all child-care responsibilities. Nine-tenths said they found looking after the children tiring, and a lot of the mothers said that child-care was harder work than going out to work.

Do you think caring for children within the family is seen as an important task? Do you think people who choose to spend time caring for their children are respected and looked up to by others? How could more people be brought to understand how important it is to recognise

Average time on child-care tasks during the day

	minutes per day
getting children up and dressed	38
taking to toilet and changing nappies (day and night)	39
taking to child minder, nursery or school and collecting	35
extra time for shopping	29
extra time for meals (cooking, serving, washing up)	119
washing and bathing	43
putting to bed	38
extra time for washing and ironing	34
clearing up and cleaning after children	48
all tasks	**423**

Figure 10

the value of this work? In what other ways might fathers be involved with their children's care? Does this evidence make you wish to change anything about these situations?

Although many people are forced to try, it is clearly impossible for someone to do all these essential child-care tasks and also go out to work without a great deal of reliable help.

One child-care task

Have you ever changed a baby's nappy? With modern products such as nappy liners, disposable nappies, and nappy cleaning agents this is an easier task than it used to be. However, it has to be repeated many times and uses up several hours each week. Parents often try to make this time happier by taking the chance to play some tickling games with the baby and to talk to the baby.

Unusually dry nappies or unusually dirty ones can be the first signs of illness in babies. Too much loss of liquid, as with diarrhoea, can be dangerous for a baby.

Use a babywear catalogue, the information leaflets you sent for, and some real nappies to help you to find out about different sorts of nappies and associated products. Try to practise folding a towelling nappy in several different ways on a large doll. Look up the cost of the different sorts of nappies and try to find out about a nappy delivery service. (Most babies get through roughly four or five nappies per day.) How should disposable nappies be disposed of? How should towelling nappies be cleaned and dried? Estimate the comparative costs of using different kinds of nappies.

What factors might influence a family to choose one sort of nappy? In what sorts of situations might disposable nappies be particularly useful? Many families use a variety of types of nappy; for example, they might use a towelling nappy at night and disposable nappies during the day. Why do you think this is?

Pennies and pounds

What sort of things should you include if you want to work out how much it costs to have a baby? Make a list and cost out several items from your list based on buying from different places and also allowing for making things, buying second-hand, and presents.
Would you include maternity clothes and clothes for the mum to wear while she is breast-feeding and getting back her shape?
What about the cost of a washing machine, a tumble drier, a car, or heating the room in which the baby spends most time?
Will the mother be going back to work or will the family lose her income?

Of course there will probably be a few savings. The mother will receive free prescriptions and dental care until the baby is one year old. She may also receive Maternity Benefits and she will receive Child Benefit each month. Your local Social Security Office will be able to tell you more about these. Might there be any other savings?

Parents want to do the best they can for their baby. Is it always best to spend money on buying new things? Do new parents usually have a great deal of money to spend?

Set up a display of several pieces of equipment, clothing, and toys for a baby. Now look at each article and decide whether it would be essential to have and if it is whether as a new parent you would buy it new or second-hand. Maybe you could make something like it or maybe it would be a suitable thing to ask for as a present. If you decide to buy it second-hand what sort of safety points would it be important to check? What do you really feel about buying things second-hand for babies? Are there any ways in which second-hand goods can be made more desirable? If setting up a display of real articles is impossible for you to do, then use your catalogue to prepare a poster.

There is a great deal of pressure on new parents to buy, buy, buy! Do babies need all the things that are advertised? Will they be worse off if their parents decide not to buy them all these things?

Creative coping

Empty plastic ice cream and margarine tubs with lids can be very useful. Can you find out the sort of things a family with babies or small children might use them for?

There are several bags on the market designed to be especially useful to parents when changing babies. Examine one of these and write a list of its most important features. Can you now make a similar bag for less money?

Other articles you can make enjoyably and cheaply include duvet covers, cot bumpers, soft toys, rattles, mobiles, and friezes.

Now try these

There is a lot to remember when you first start to look after a new baby.

Explain why the following are important things to do. Can you also give any hints on how to do these either economically and/or with pleasure?

the baby should be cuddled and talked to a lot
the baby must be kept warm
the baby must be safe
the baby must be fed approximately every four hours.

Try looking at some things literally from the baby's point of view by actually putting yourself in the same position, for example, on the floor. What do babies see when adults pick them up, when they are in their prams, or when they are lying on a blanket on the floor?

All babies can do is eat, sleep, cry, and do dirty nappies.

Explain whether this is true or false. If someone believes this how might it cause them to behave towards a baby?

That baby really had it in for me from the minute it was born.

Can this be true? Why might a parent feel like this?

There is a lot of pressure on expectant parents to spend a great deal of money. Can you say where these pressures come from? What do you think they make new parents feel like? How can new parents be helped to cope with these feelings?

Make a collage out of all the baby pictures you collected and beside this write a list of the sort of information that has been left out of this public view of babies.

Make space in your life for your baby.

What sort of space do you think this means? Can you give several different examples?

The arrival of a new baby is a special event. We all find unusual and special events stressful, however happy the occasion might be. In what ways can stress show itself? What signs of stress might the following sometimes show?
the mother of a bride
a boyfriend going out with a girl for the first time
grandparents having grandchildren to stay in their house
the father of a new baby.

SEE ALSO

Childcarers for more about organising the care of babies and young children.
Feelings and behaviour includes more ideas about what influences there are on us and what we can do about them.

See the book *Textiles for People* (in this series) for more information on making fabric articles for children.

"The British Way of Birth" (published by Pan, 1982, with an introduction by Esther Rantzen) will give you a lot of real accounts of parents' feelings.

Thomas's First 300 Days and *Thomas Till Three* (Kestrel Books, 1984), by Thomas Bergman, show in pictures how a baby changes and develops during this time.

Which? magazine (March 1978) investigated nappies. You can ask to see a copy of this at your local reference library.

Try to invite a mother and/or father to come and bath or feed their baby with you. What sort of advance preparation do you think you should make?

Perhaps a few of you could visit a club for toddlers and their parents and report back on what you see, and what you think the advantages are of these to the parents and to the small babies and toddlers. It may also be possible to arrange time with parents and young children in other situations, for example; well-baby clinics.

Books and television

Collect a copy of next week's *Radio Times* and *TV Times*.
Write to your local library asking if you can visit the children's section, as a group.
Send for information from the Letterbox Library and Tapeworm (addresses on pages 177 and 180).

Use and misuse

Carry out a survey of your own and other people's use of books, magazines, newpapers, television, and radio. What sort of things would it be important to find out?

Look through the television and radio programmes for next week and plan what, if anything, you would like to view or listen to each day. Can you say why you chose these programmes? Try to group your programmes so that you can see how much of each type you will watch and listen to. How many hours might you spend watching television or listening to the radio next week? Now plan the programmes that a 4-year-old might enjoy next week. How could you use a video or tape recorder to help a young child enjoy these programmes more?

> Television makes children lazy.

> Children do not read as much as they used to.

> Television is just a background noise.

> Children see things they should not see on Television.

Some people feel very strongly about television. What do you think? Can you point to any good things young children might gain from watching television? You might start by looking at the sort of reading television actually encourages.

Children's television

Use the published programme guides to work out how many minutes of young children's television there are each week. What time of day are these programmes on? Why do you think the programme planners put them on at this time?

Using a video recorder record a selection of these programmes and then review them. As you are watching them ask yourself these sorts of questions: Can you see any signs of them trying to make learning fun? Do they try to teach new skills and new words? Are they entertaining and do they encourage careful listening and watching? Do they try to link what they do to the child's life? Do they also teach the children about other lifestyles and things they would not normally see? Why is it very important that television programmes should not present a one-sided view of society? Did the children's television programmes you watched include examples of people from lots of different groups in our society?

Now make a checklist against which you would mark a children's television programme for a 5-year-old. Do you think there would be any advantage to a parent in doing what you have just done before letting their children see the programmes?

Can you remember what you watched on television last week?

Remembering and learning are always quite difficult things to do but they are easier if one is doing something active, just watching or listening is not enough. What sort of active participation do children's television programmes encourage? In what ways do you think these activities help the children to learn and remember? How would talking to a child about what they watch on television or listen to on the radio help in a child's learning?

Plan a television or radio programme of your own for under 5-year-olds. It should be no more than fifteen minutes long and it should encourage them to take part actively. What will you do to make sure that it is suitable and enjoyable?

Violence

Some young children stay up after nine o'clock at night and watch programmes which are really intended for adults. This means that they will see things which were only thought suitable for adults, such as scary or violent stories and examples of adult relationships. There has been a large amount of research on the viewing of violence on television. However, people still disagree about this. Judge some programmes for yourself. Start by thinking about what each of you considers to be violent. Is some violence worse than other sorts of violence? What does this depend on? Could it depend on things like whether the people are equals or not, how real the violence seems, or how close to home it is? Do you think that some violence is acceptable?

Do you think it might be undesirable for a young child to see any of the examples of violence in figure 11 (over the page)? If so, how would you prevent them from doing so?

Figure 11 Examples of violence.
  a) Cartoon type.
  b) Fictional but realistic incident from a television serial.
  c) Daily news incident seen on television or in a newspaper.

Children's books

Libraries

What have the libraries in colour pictures 1 and 2 (between pages 72 and 73) done to make books more attractive to small children?
 Libraries often issue booklists with ideas for children of all ages. If you were the librarian writing this list what sort of things would you take into consideration when recommending books for children between the ages of three and five years old? Remember children of this age only experience the things we introduce them to, so this is a very good opportunity to show that everyone in our society should have equal opportunities and respect. This applies particularly to those who have in the past been treated unequally. (Use the information from the Letterbox Library to help you to spot what to look out for.)

Try out your list of things to consider against a number of children's books recommended for this age range.

What sorts of books would you recommend for people of your own age? Try to make sure that your list contains a variety of different types of books on different subjects. Would any of your points to consider for young children's books apply to this list too?

Make your own

Books intended for adults to use normally have a great deal of printing on each page and few illustrations. But children's books often have large print, bright colours, few words put in interesting places, repeated phrases, pictures continued over the page, flaps to push and pull, doors and windows that open, and things to find or feel. These make a book more lively for the child.

Make a story book for a 3-year-old. Keep the story simple but interesting. Your book will be read to the child by an adult, but the writing should be fairly large and very clear. A word processor would be a great help in doing this. What else should you think about when making this book? The appearance of your book should tempt the child to ask for it to be read to them. Some home-made books are shown in figure 12.

Why is it important that children's books are particularly strong?

Figure 12
A selection of home-made books.

Sharing is enjoying

Books and television programmes can provide the beginnings of new experiences. They can also back up and extend things which have actually happened to the child. They can encourage children to use their imagination and they can be fun. They can prepare children for new situations, for example going to hospital, the arrival of a new baby, etc. Children need adults to introduce them to books and television. They need to learn that written words "say" things, and that words and pictures help each other.

Choose a book, a television or radio programme, a story or cassette tape for a young child and suggest how you could:
encourage discussion
link what you are seeing to the child's own experiences
turn something from the book or programme into an activity you could do together.

Now try these

Read a few pages of a child's book aloud into a tape recorder. Does your voice sound interesting? Could you add any sound effects?

Look at a selection of young children's books from the library and carry out a survey on what sort of writing there is in them, the size and shape of the writing, the amount there is on each page, and where it is on the page. Can you find any examples of the words and the illustrations being used in interesting ways together? This is called the "layout" of a page.

When was the last time you really enjoyed a book, radio or television programme, video, video game, or computer program? What was it about? What did you enjoy about it? Share your enjoyment with a friend by telling them about it.

In which rooms in your home are books, magazines, newspapers, radios, and the television kept? Do you use them in these rooms?

Plan a book for a 3-year-old who is going to be starting playgroup soon, or for a 4-year-old who is going to be starting school soon.
Children like to hear stories about themselves. Try to include helpful information so that the child will know what to expect.

> My 4-year-old is not allowed to watch television after 5.30 p.m. If we lay down firm guidelines about viewing when children are young they will become discriminating, critical viewers as they get older.

Can you explain what these parents mean? Do you think that they are right?

There are several different ways to get books for children. What are the advantages and disadvantages of some of these methods?
library
library van
loan to mother and toddler club from a library
book clubs
jumble sales
buy from a book shop
buy from a shop like a supermarket or chain store
borrow from a friend
make your own

Suggest at least five ways in which adults can help children make the best use of books, television, and radio.

If possible, carry out an assessment of a computer program intended for use with young children. Is it very easy to load and use? What is your opinion of the notes that come with it? Is it rewarding to use? Does it encourage any learning whilst still being fun to do?

Take a short children's book and record it yourself onto cassette. So that the child can follow the story in the book do not forget to include a "bleep" of some sort to tell the child to turn the page! What can you do to make this recording extra special that a manufacturer cannot do?

Find as many different lists as you can of recommendations of books for children of a certain age. You can find these in libraries, catalogues, book shops, and from book clubs. Try to have a look at a selection of these books. Why do you think they are particularly suitable for children of this age?

Try to visit a library and watch the young children and adults using the books. Write a report on what you see.

Make a poster to display at a well-baby clinic to encourage parents to read to their children. What sort of things might be stopping them from doing this very often?

SEE ALSO

Talking for more ideas on encouraging young children to enjoy language of all sorts.

For more information on computer programs for very young children write to AUCBE, ESM, and Ebury Software (addresses on pages 175–176).
The Good Book Guide to Children's Books (Penguin, 1985), *Puffins for Parents* (Penguin, 1984) and the magazine *Books for your children* (Ragdoll Productions Ltd), all have lots of ideas for making books interesting for children from birth to thirteen years old.

Celebrations

 Collect some happy memories of childhood celebrations. What do you remember most about these occasions?

What can we celebrate?

Among the things people celebrate are religious occasions, weekends, holidays, birthdays, special achievements and events, and seeing friends or relatives after a long absence.

In small groups try to give several examples of some of these sorts of occasions.

What sorts of events have you celebrated recently?

How can we celebrate?

We can celebrate by giving cards and presents, coming together for special meals, swopping roles in the house, singing special songs and telling traditional stories, joining in a religious ceremony together, putting on special clothes, decorating the house, and using the best cutlery and crockery. There may also be fêtes or parades.

Some of these, like the ones in figures 13 and 14, are small celebrations which happen often.

Figure 13 Breakfast in bed together.

Figure 14 Let's have a takeaway.

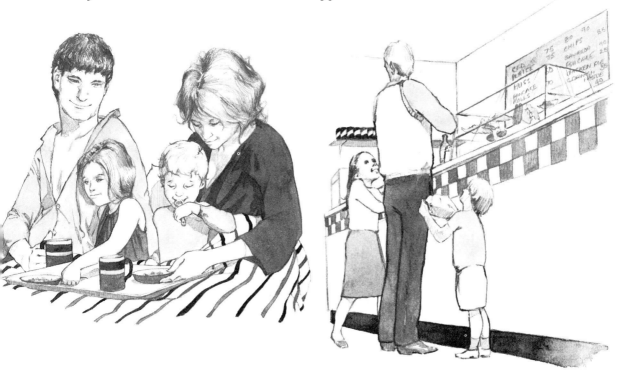

Figure 15 Happy Birthday!

There are also occasions we celebrate every year, as in figure 15. Some things we celebrate less often, as in figure 16.

Why is it important to celebrate?

Celebrations should be enjoyable, relaxing, and reassuring. They can strengthen our religious faith and renew values which are different from our everyday ones. They can give us time off to think about our lives and to enjoy a different side of life. They often mark important historical or personal events we do not wish to forget. They divide the year up for us and make some days special.

Make a calendar for next year and write on it all the events you are going to celebrate!

What sort of things would someone be missing if they did not celebrate anything at all?

Many people celebrate regularly on one day of each week. Do you know any families who make one day each week a little bit different and special? Why do you think they do this? How do they make this day pleasant?

Which is your favourite occasion to celebrate? What do you especially like about this event?

Figure 16 Getting married.

Successful celebrations

Most celebrations rely on some sort of organisation being carried out. This can be very simple, such as making or buying a card and giving it with a bunch of flowers and a kiss. Or the organisation can be so complicated that you pay for people to help you with it, such as for a wedding.

What sort of companies are there to help with the organisation for a wedding? Why are some families very keen on doing as much of the preparation as they can themselves?

Most celebrations do not have to be expensive. In fact, it is often the thought and the trouble which someone has gone to which makes an event particularly successful. However some occasions will be costly.

What sort of traditional arrangements are there to help with the cost of these important, expensive celebrations?

Is it important that everyone enjoys a celebration? (This can be difficult if there is a wide age range of people present, or if all the work falls to one person.)

What sort of planning can be done in advance to make sure everyone has a good time?

The anticipation, preparation, and practising of special skills such as dancing, cooking, or speech-making all build up to a climax, and all the members of the family want to join in. Young children like to feel that they are an important part of the family, so if they can contribute in some small way to the special atmosphere they will enjoy it all the more. They also gain a great deal from having happy memories of these events. Taking part in celebrations helps children to have a strong sense of family and community.

Different celebrations

Different groups in our society celebrate different events. Here are just a few examples:

In the practice of Islam Muslims have the religious Festival of Fast Breaking (Fid-Ul-Fitr), which is celebrated at the end of the fast of Ramadan. This is a very happy time when people wear their best or new clothes and families go to the Mosque to say prayers. As an important part of this celebration the poorer members of the community are helped by the wealthier ones. People visit each other and give cards. There are parties and special meals and the children are given presents.

Passover is a very important event celebrated by Jewish people in March or April. It marks the time when the Jews fled from Egypt. It is said that there wasn't enough time for the bread to rise, and so the people took unleavened, flat bread with them. Today all food with yeast in it is taken out of the house at this time of the year. As a light-hearted part of the symbolic Passover meal parents often hide small pieces of bread for the young children to find. The family also uses special crockery and utensils to eat this meal together, and there are special religious services in the synagogue.

Sikhs celebrate the life and work of particular gurus on special days of the year. (The word Sikh means "disciple", and the word guru means "teacher".) In January there is a festival to remember the birthday of Guru Gobind Singh. This is celebrated by having a complete reading of the holy book and a ceremony of worship in the gurdwara, and a special meal together.

On Shrove Tuesday Christian people in Great Britain run pancake races and eat pancakes for their tea. This is because during Lent certain foods were forbidden and the cooking of pancakes used up the remains of these foods. This was the last opportunity for enjoying oneself for several weeks and entertainments like races used to take place.

Chinese people celebrate the start of the Chinese New Year in a very lively and colourful way, with processions through the streets of people dressed as dragons. (See colour picture 3, between pages 72 and 73.) The Chinese also make lanterns, cards and kites, eat special foods, and "spring clean".

West Indians have a festival called Carnival. Steel bands play in the streets and there are firework displays and processions for which people prepare very elaborate costumes and headpieces.

The above are very brief descriptions and to learn more you might be able to ask someone from your school or an outside speaker to talk to you about how their ethnic group or religion celebrates. Celebrations can be very significant to individuals and groups of people. They are often a serious and important part of their faith.

You might also be able to see the public Chinese or West Indian celebrations in a city near you or on the television news.

Birthday parties

When people travel to live in another country they often take their celebrations with them. Your own birthday would probably be an occasion you would wish to celebrate in some way wherever you were. It is an important occasion for young children too, and they often have a birthday party.

What do you need to consider when you are planning a birthday party for a small child? You could think about how long the party will be, how many children you will invite, and how you will prevent the birthday child becoming overexcited and upset.

With a friend make a checklist of the points you think it important to consider when planning a child's party.

The sort of activities you plan for very young children should be fairly simple. Young children enjoy games and songs they are familiar with, such as pass the parcel and nursery rhymes. If you are going to give prizes everyone has to get one: children of this age are not able to cope with the disappointment of feeling left out.

The food should be easy to eat with small fingers, and be in very small portions. The birthday cake itself can be great fun to do and not too difficult if you use moulding icing which you can colour and shape as you want. To what extent do you think the food at children's birthday parties should meet the nutritional guidelines?

How could you make tiny and attractive portions of several different sorts of foods? What sort of cutters and containers could you use?

You can also organise a child's party with a theme such as a circus or a zoo party. In a small group choose a theme and show how you would use it for the invitations, the children's clothes, the room decorations, the food, and the party activities.

The children are also often given something to take home with them. Can you suggest three inexpensive but enjoyable items for this?

Now try these

Describe an occasion you have enjoyed celebrating. Was there any organisation involved? If so, what was done and who did it?

You receive an invitation to a wedding which says "No young children". Why do you think the couple want this? What are your feelings about this?

Young children enjoy joining in the preparation for a celebration. Choose an occasion to celebrate, and with a few friends make a collection of activities for young children to do called "Getting ready to celebrate". Make clear what sort of adult preparation would be needed before each activity. You could include ideas for making invitation cards, table and room decorations, simple cookery, small presents, and perhaps also making articles ready for playing games such as a picture of a donkey and a tail for "Pin the tail on the donkey".

Choose a small occasion you would like to celebrate and draw up a plan of organisation. Pay particular attention as to who does what and to how much time you have.

Parents are often grateful for help at a children's party so you might be able to use what you have learned. You could advertise your services at a local playgroup! Plan what you would include in this advertisement.

Invite someone who is about to or who has just got married to come and tell you about the organisation and preparation.

Make a poster or frieze which could be put up in a playgroup or nursery school, showing the children the excitement of different ethnic and religious festivals.

SEE ALSO

Food and drink will give you more information about the nutritional guidelines.
Playing will help you to understand more about the sorts of activities young children enjoy.

"Celebrations" is a booklet giving details of a number of festivals and suggestions on how to participate in them. It is available from The Beeches School (address on page 175).
Festivals in World Religions (Longman, 1986), edited by Alan Brown, is a useful reference book.
There is a series of books called "Celebrations", published by A & C Black in 1985.

Childcarers

Collect a number of pictures of different sorts of people from magazines. Try to make sure that you have included a good mixture of people of different ages and types; remember that everyone needs caring for in some way.

Send for information on home safety from your district Health Education/Promotion Unit (see page 174). They will also be able to let you have some leaflets about childminders whose job it is to care for other people's babies and small children. Remember that it is not enough to just know a lot about safety: you also need to care about it so that you use your knowledge. Write to Help the Aged (address on page 177) for information about caring for the elderly.

How to care

Being able to show care and consideration for other people in a thoughtful way is a very strong quality. Bullies are weak people.

Some people show they care in ways that are difficult to understand. Who cares most: the teacher who says "Oh, forget your homework" or the teacher who says "That piece of homework is important and I want it handed in by Tuesday"? Can you think of any other examples where somebody shows that they care but in a fairly tough way?

Using your pictures of all sorts of different people, try to say what sort of care each of them might need. The information you receive from Help the Aged will help you with this.

Toddler topples book-case

Four-year-old Maria pulled a half-built book-case down on her and her younger brother while her father had popped out to buy some extra nails. 'I had just run out of nails, and the shop was only next door, so I thought I'd just pop out and get some. I didn't think the kids could come to any harm just for a few minutes,' said their father.

BABY BURNT WHILE MUM 'POPS OUT'

Sarah Jane Davies was left alone for only a few minutes, but it was long enough for her to burn her hands on an electric fire. 'I was only on the doorstep' said Mrs Davies.

Figure 17

SIX-YEAR-OLD IN BEACH DRAMA

Six-year-old Paul Lloyd had a narrow escape yesterday when he was swept out to sea by a sudden wave. His father, John Lloyd, had left him on his own while he went to help his daughter, Sophie, put on her arm bands. 'I thought he'd be alright for a few minutes. I just didn't realise how quickly these big waves can suddenly appear.'

Figure 17 (continued)

Looking after children

What is special about caring for small children?

Why do children need constant care and protection? How could the types of accidents shown in figure 17 have been prevented?

Why do you think adults are sometimes tempted to go out without arranging for someone else to come and look after their children?

If a child left alone in a house came to any harm then the parents would be liable to prosecution by the police.

Babysitters

Parents often ask responsible teenagers to look after their young children while they go out.

What have been your and your friends' experiences of babysitting? Compare notes with each other. What rates of pay did you receive, what information were you given, what difficulties did you have, and how well did you know the children you looked after? How do you think the children felt?

These are some of the reasons people do babysitting; to earn money; because they enjoy being trusted with the children; because they like being with the children; because they meet other people; because they can rely on having a good babysitter back; and because they feel their help is needed and appreciated.

What might be **your** most important reasons for doing babysitting?

If you were an adult choosing a babysitter what would you look for? Write a list of important points. Now write a postcard advertisement to go in a newsagent's window mentioning your main points. What would you do when people rang you up about the job? How would you find out whether they were suitable? What other ways are there of finding a babysitter?

If you were the person applying for the job as a babysitter what would you want to know about the family, the house, and the job? What arrangements could you make for meeting and getting to know the children? What safety points would you ask about?

Being a good babysitter

Here is a list of things you might need to be able to do if you are going to be good at babysitting babies and very small children:

change a nappy
give a bottle feed
sing several nursery rhymes
tell a story
know several quiet games to play
be able to be firm without being nasty
know some basic First Aid
understand and care about safety with young children
know when you need help
be able to talk to adults clearly and politely

Give yourself a star-rating from one to four, depending on how good you are at doing these. Which do you need to find out more about before you do any babysitting? How could you do this?

What might you need to add to this list for someone babysitting older children?

We need a babysitter

Read the account from an interview below; and see if you agree with the parents. It is with a mum and a dad who are part of a babysitting circle. The babysitting circle is organised like this; a large group of parents who live quite near each other circulate a list of their names and telephone numbers saying they are willing to babysit for each other. (Sometimes this list also says things like "I cannot babysit on Tuesday nights because I go to an evening class".) Each family start with sixteen tokens. No money is used at all, and any new family joining the scheme is given sixteen tokens to start them off. You pay one token per hour to the person who babysits for you, and you can earn tokens by babysitting for other people. When you need a babysitter you telephone anyone on the list.

MUM   "I feel much happier knowing that my children are being looked after by someone who knows how to cope because they have children of their own. It

	means I don't need to worry, I can forget about them and have a good night out."
DAD	"It also means that we can stay out later than if we had a teenager sitting; but we do have to do babysitting in return and some nights, for instance New Year's Eve, all our circle want to go out so it is difficult to get a sitter then."
MUM	"I don't like my neighbours knowing so much about us but it is a cheaper way of organising things."
INTERVIEWER	Which do your children prefer?"
DAD	"Well, when they were little I think they preferred having an adult that they knew quite well but now they quite enjoy having a teenager who is prepared to play with them a bit."
MUM	"Adults are much more understanding if you come back an hour or so late. It is awful to have to say 'Well, we must go now because of the babysitter' just when you are beginning to enjoy yourself".
DAD	"But it costs us double tokens after 12 o'clock which means one of us has to do quite a lot of babysitting to make up the time."
MUM	"It is also a bit of work for the organiser of the circle getting new members and issuing lists of who is in the circle and the nights when they would prefer not to babysit."
INTERVIEWER	"Are there ever any difficulties with people taking advantage of the system?"
MUM	"There was a problem last year when some of the people on the list stopped sitting because their children had got old enough to look after themselves, and we had to find new people to join. But on the whole it works quite well because we all know that we have to make it work".
DAD	"We did have a problem with our children not wanting to have one or two of the parents babysit for them but we just avoided ringing those particular people up when we needed a sitter. You do need to be quite well organised."

What are the advantages and disadvantages of this system of babysitting?

Childminders

Some parents need their children looked after for longer periods of time, either because the family is a lone parent one, or because both parents work or go to college, perhaps.

Sometimes one parent will go out to work in the evenings when the other parent can look after the children, or one of them might go out to work early in the morning and a relative might look after the children for a while. Occasionally the mother or father might be able to do their work at home, but usually if they are working or studying both parents will need to be out for most of the day and then they might arrange for a childminder to look after their children.

Do young children need their parents, especially their mother, all the time if they are to grow up healthy and happy? There is a lot of argument about this, but recent research seems to show that a young child can handle several relationships very well. However, if both parents are exhausted after working long hours and have little time or energy left for their children, or if they feel that it is wrong to go to work while their children are young, then this *will* be harmful to the child.

Some of the most important points for the parents to consider when choosing a childminder are:

How easily available is the childminder?
Will the childminder be able to look after your child for the months or years ahead?
What is the home like?
Is the home safe for a child this age?
What sort of relationship would your child have with the adult?
What sort of things would the child do during a typical day at the childminders?
Would the childminder be able to take your child to the clinic for the normal development checks?
Is the childminder well informed, and perhaps even trained, in the needs of young children?

All childminders must be registered with the local authority.
Here is a list of several other ways of arranging reliable, adequate care for children.

A nanny who either lives in or who comes every day is another alternative; but they can be expensive because they have often done several years of training. Occasionally families can share a nanny which makes the cost more reasonable.

There are also a few local authority nurseries which care for young children all day; but these would not provide a one-to-one relationship for the child, or a home atmosphere.

There are a few companies which provide childcare facilities and flexible work hours for both male and female employees with young children.

Part-time work is not usually as well paid as full-time work, and this is why some people now "share a job" between two. They might also arrange to share the care of their children.

In pairs, decide on five important things to look for when choosing all-day care for very young childen. Now rate some of the above methods, according to how far they satisfy your priorities.

Foster families

Occasionally families need their children looked after for a rather longer period of time, because they have difficulties which they cannot cope with by themselves. The length of time can vary from a week, to months, or even years. Fostering is a way of continuing to provide a family life for children who, for various reasons, cannot live with their own families for a while. This may be because of the breakdown of a marriage, a sudden death, illness, or perhaps housing problems. The Local Authority Social Services department takes over the responsibilities of the parents. They then try to find the right foster family. These families treat the children as if they were their own, and they often also help to keep the children in contact with their own families, especially if there is a good chance that the children will be returning to them. Foster parents are usually trained, helped, and paid to do this very difficult and special job.

Why do you think that nearly all children who are in care say they prefer to be in foster families rather than in children's homes?

Now try these

Carry out a survey to find out how many of your friends do babysitting. Do they tend to be boys or girls? How much are they paid? How well prepared are they to do a good job? Do the adults give them all the necessary information and help? What else do you think it would be important to find out about? Present your findings as clearly as possible.

Prepare a form that can be reproduced requesting information from parents so that you can ask them to fill it in next time you babysit. You will want to know where you can reach the parents, and where the nearest available adult is; but what else would you need to know?

Prepare a noticeboard full of information about being a good babysitter so that all your friends are as well-informed as you.

A well-run babysitting agency could be very useful to the parents of young children in your area. These are some of the things you would have to think about if you set up such an agency: advertising, training, allocation of work, rates of pay, reliability, references. Take one of these areas and explain how you would organise it.

Read the Health Education/Promotion Unit's information on home safety that you collected and then suggest ten points you would include in a Babysitters' Safety Code.

Ask a local social worker to tell you about one child who was fostered with a family, or look in a national or local newspaper and read a description of a child who is looking for a foster family. What difficulties do you think anyone would have when joining a new family like this?

> *People should not have children if they are not prepared to stay at home and look after them themselves.*

Do you agree with this point of view?

What sort of help do you think could be available to parents to ensure that fewer families feel the need to have their children taken into care for even a short period of time?

> *If a child has to be taken into care the best place is in another family where the child can benefit from all the normal advantages of family life.*

What do you think these advantages are?

> When I went to collect Sally from playschool the other day there was a teacher, a painter, a doctor, a secretary, a pharmacist, an electrician, and a laboratory technician waiting to collect their children! Can this country really afford to train these people and then not have them work full time?

Large numbers of both men and women now go on to further education. The years during which they stay at home to bring up their children cost this country money. Do you think this is money well spent? Could we organise things differently?

SEE ALSO

Families for more information about the sort of care families provide for their members.

Children have rights

Send for information from Oxfam, UNICEF, and the NSPCC, who publish a great deal about the lives of children. (Addresses on pages 175–180.)
Collect a number of opinions by listing the statements you and other people use to complete the sentence "Every child in the world has the right to . . . . . .".

The right to . . .

Now you have a list of rights you and others think every child in the world is entitled to, compare your thoughts with "The Declaration of the Rights of the Child" which the United Nations General Assembly decided on in 1959.

1) The right to equality, regardless of race, religion, sex, or nationality.
2) The right to healthy mental and physical development.
3) The right to a name and a nationality.
4) The right to sufficient food, housing, and medical care.
5) The right to special care if handicapped.
6) The right to love, understanding, and care.
7) The right to free education, play, and recreation.
8) The right to immmediate aid in the event of disaster and emergencies.
9) The right to protection from cruelty, neglect, and exploitation.
10) The right to protection from persecution and to an upbringing in the spirit of worldwide brotherhood and peace.

Do you agree that every child is entitled as of right to these things?
  Clearly not all children are lucky enough to get their basic rights. Can you think of any examples of children both in Great Britain and other countries who are or who have been denied any of these rights?
  The basic needs of children are the same all over the world, but these needs can be met in many different ways and we have to take care that we do not consider some children to be deprived just because they do not have what we might think of as toys or nice clothes. Every culture has its own songs, games, toys, and ways of dressing. Some more simple societies than ours can be more successful in bringing up their children. We find it difficult to introduce children to the adult world of work because work has become so separated from the rest of our lives. Children very rarely know and understand what their parents do at work in our society. Whereas in a simpler society they can often enjoy helping their parents at work from a young age.

Figure 18 These pupils, from the Cherwell School, Oxford, are painting the biggest jigsaw in the world. This was part of the "walk for the world" which was arranged to lobby the Government over Third World issues and to raise money through sponsorship.

Difficulties

However strongly we believe that all children are entitled to the best treatment, we also have to face up to some practical difficulties. Sometimes it is very difficult for us to provide children with what they need in order to grow up healthily.

It is very disturbing that there is such unequal provision for children in different parts of the world.

Many people believe that it is the duty of all of us to try to make sure that all this world's children receive good care. So do the children in figure 18.

They say that they feel their own life would be improved if they knew no child in the world went without these basic rights. They mean that they would then feel freer to enjoy their own lives. Would you be prepared to have less so that this situation could come about?

Take one of the United Nation Rights and in a small group try to list the sorts of things that you think might be stopping some children from receiving this right.

A child survival revolution

There is surprisingly very little relationship between the Gross National Product of a country (which is one way of saying how wealthy a country is) and the number of young children who die in that country. This is because the wealth of a country is sometimes shared amongst only a very few people.

If the money available is not shared out fairly there will be injustices in the sort of care people receive. In Great Britain, for instance, the care that a premature baby receives varies widely depending on where that baby was born, and in a country like Nigeria some of the people are very wealthy whilst others starve.

UNICEF believes that the world has the means to halve the number of children who die.

There are five inexpensive things which could be done straight away to ensure more children survive:

1 Immunisation is not expensive and it could save many more children in the developing world from death or disability from the six most dangerous diseases: measles, whooping cough, tetanus, TB, diphtheria, and polio. At present only about a fifth of these children are immunised. The children in Great Britain are only protected because nearly every child is immunised.

2 More babies die in poor countries if they are bottle fed than if they are breast fed. This is because the water used might not be clean, and the baby milk powder might not be used in the correct quantities. Breast-feeding is more hygienic, more nutritious, and it provides small babies with some resistance to infections. Many countries have now banned all advertising of dried milk products, specially for babies. Not all mothers feel able to breast-feed, although there is a great deal of evidence to show that it is better for their babies. Why do you think they feel like this?

3 In Great Britain growth charts are used to check on the healthy development of babies. These give a warning if the child is not developing normally. If all young children were weighed regularly and had their weight put on a simple chart it would be obvious immediately if the child were being malnourished, and action could be taken. Recent cases of child abuse in Great Britain have shown that if these development checks are not carried out warning signs can be missed.

4 The most common cause of death amongst babies in poorer countries is dehydration, caused by the child having diarrhoea and losing too much liquid. This liquid is not just water: it is a complicated mixture of water and mineral salts, but it can be successfully replaced by drinking a simple mixture of sugar, salt, and clean water. Very inexpensive sachets of a mixture of glucose and salt are now produced to be used in these countries. It is also a simple matter to check that this is needed by a small baby because when they are dehydrated the fontanelle on the top of their head sinks in, and this can be felt by the parents. This is very serious but as long as it is spotted early enough the cure is usually a simple one. Diarrhoea is dangerous for all small babies and it is possible to buy a product in the chemists which will replace body salts and fluid.

5 Good ante-natal care is also essential to giving babies a good start in life, and children are more likely to survive if their parents leave at least a year between having one child and the next. This is mainly because the mother will then have a chance to regain her own health. However, parents only seem willing to do this if they are convinced that their children stand a reasonable chance of survival. Families do seem willing to limit their birth rates, however, if they are confident that their children will not die. In Great Britain there is still quite a lot of work to do to ensure that all pregnant women attend ante-natal clinics. Why do you think some women do not go?

In Great Britain

There are many families with young children in Great Britain whose incomes fall below the level of Supplementary Benefit. This means that the families do not have enough money to meet their basic needs. What are these "basic needs"?

Babies stand less chance of survival even in Great Britain if their parents are poor or if they live in certain areas. Why do you think this is so?

There are many children at risk in Great Britain. The NSPCC estimates that one child a week dies from injuries inflicted by its parents or guardians, and there are many more who are mistreated. Why is this still happening?

Child abuse is not new. Dr Barnardo's and The National Society for the Prevention of Cruelty to Children were both founded in the nineteenth century because so many children needed protection then. And even today there are many newspaper reports of children being badly treated; but this could mean that the reporters are being more vigilant, and not that more children are suffering. However, many parents are under a great deal of stress and pressure today and this can result in them finding it difficult to cope with their children. Parents normally want to look after and protect their children, talk to them, and play with them, but if the parents are unhappy or unwell and receive little support from those around them they might find it difficult to build a close relationship with their baby. This can harm their ability to protect and care for their child. When cases of child abuse are taken to court and a parent is found guilty do you think the blame is all theirs?

If children are entitled to certain things as of right they should receive them no matter what. Children do not have to earn loving, caring parents, and a stable background with enough to eat. What could be done to make sure that more children receive these things?

There have been reports which suggest that some parents lack the basic information and skills they need to look after children well. What evidence is there to suggest this might be true? What sorts of things do these parents not know about? When and how could they be given

Mankind owes to the child the best it has to give.

opportunities to learn these things? Can you think of anything that might prevent them from starting to learn them?

Now try these

What sort of things does this mean? Why do you think children deserve the best treatment possible?

Choose one of the UN's Rights of the Child and explain why it is so important. What sort of things might prevent a child having this right fulfilled?

To what extent did you and your friends receive these Rights of the Child when you were young children?

What can people (including you) do to try to ensure that more children receive more of the rights they are entitled to in the future?

The National Association for Young People In Care and the Child Poverty Action Group see it as part of their rôle to try to ensure that the people they are concerned about receive their basic rights. Try to find out more about these organisations and the people they represent.

SEE ALSO

Diseases and immunisation for more about this important area of preventative medicine.

See the book *Home and Consumer* (in this series) for more about children's rights, in the Topic "Responsibilities".

Clothes

Collect some information about what today's children are wearing by looking at the young children around you.
Send for some children's wear catalogues from companies such as Mothercare (address on page 178), and collect some ideas about what children used to wear from history books and old family photographs.

Getting dressed

Clothes can be frustrating and uncomfortable things for babies and young children and they enjoy having no clothes on at all (figure 19).

Figure 19 Does this bring back any good memories?

The sort of difficulties children have with clothes is being unable to get them done up or undone by themselves, feeling uncomfortable in them, not understanding how to get into and out of them, and feeling pulled about however carefully somebody else tries to dress them.

Can you spot how these sorts of problems have been taken account when the clothes in figure 20 were designed?

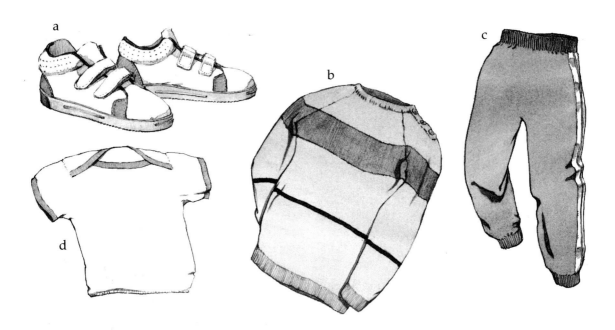

Figure 20 These make it easier to get dressed.

Look at children's clothes in catalogues and in the shops and see if you can find some more good ideas for making children's clothes comfortable to wear and easy to get on and off.

Good buys

Why do we wear clothes at all? Think of four reasons for wearing clothes and then put your reasons in order of importance.

Where did "looking good" come on your list? To whom do you think this is most important: the child or the parents?

There are certain times when it is fun for young children, both boys and girls, to get dressed up really smartly; but most of the time things like cost, comfort, and convenience are more important.

Find several garments in a catalogue (or use real children's clothes if possible) and give them star ratings according to:

1) How reasonably priced they are

2) How comfortable to wear and do things in they are

3) How convenient to look after they are.

Set your results out in a chart and give four stars if the clothes score well in any of these three areas. One star would mean that the clothes were either very expensive, uncomfortable, and difficult for a child to

Figure 21 A child's outfit.

wear happily or that you think would be difficult to keep looking clean and smart.

Guess how much you think it would cost to dress the child in figure 21. Then, using a clothes catalogue work it out as accurately as you can. How near was your guess to the real cost? Remembering that children often grow out of their clothes before they wear them out, and therefore need new clothes more often than adults, does this seem expensive to you?

In what ways do you think it might be difficult going clothes shopping with and for young children? Do you remember doing this when you were young?

Catalogues and house parties where clothes are sold are popular ways of buying children's clothes. What do you think the advantages of these two methods might be?

Comfortable clothes

Children often need their clothes to be particularly warm, waterproof, strong, flameproof, stretchy, pleasant to the touch, and quick to get on and off. Give ten examples of occasions when one or more of these qualities would be essential.

The clothes we wear can tell us what we can do happily and comfortably.

50 Clothes

Figure 22 Choosing the right clothes.

On which sort of occasions would the 4-year-old child in figure 22 be most comfortable and happy in each set of clothes?

If you comment on something someone is wearing do you automatically make a remark about the appearance of the garment such as: "That looks good"? What about saying something about the other qualities that garment might have such as: "Is it comfortable?" or "Those shoes look good for running in" or "That is the jumper Tina made you, isn't it?" or "That looks cuddly and warm". Remember that making someone look attractive is only one of the many functions clothes perform.

Favourite clothes

Children can grow to like some of their clothes a great deal. Hand-me-downs, as long as there are not too many of them and particularly if they belonged to someone special and admired, can be popular because they have pleasant associations. Clothes made especially for the child or clothes bought on special occasions or in special places can also be much loved as can particularly comfortable or easy-to-wear clothes.

There is also a lot of pleasure in making simple clothes for children. They can be made especially for the child and are sometimes economical.

The smock in colour picture 8 (between pages 72 and 73) was made from one pattern piece, the jumper was made from left-over bits of double-knitting wool, and the dress was made from a kit.

Choosing what clothes to wear and trying to get themselves dressed are important learning experiences for children. How might parents store the children's clothes in order to encourage these activities? What other sorts of encouragement could parents give? What sorts of things would the children be learning while they were doing this?

Dressing up

When children dress up and pretend to be other people they are also "trying on" different sorts of ways of behaving. They are trying to find out what it feels like to be another person. Articles like hats, cloaks, net curtains, plastic glasses, and various bags will spark off the child's imagination.

Now try these

The label in figure 23 is from an article of children's clothing. How many different pieces of information are there? Say in what way each piece of information could be useful.

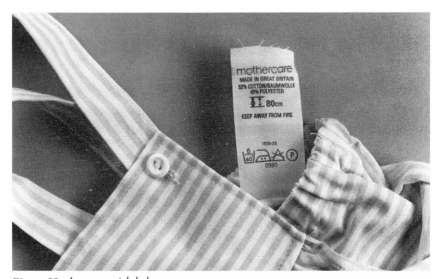

Figure 23 A garment label.

Name and explain three ways of helping to clothe a child fairly economically.

Look in a pattern book and work out the cost of making a simple child's garment yourself. How does this compare with buying something similar? Are there any other important points to consider?

Display your results with illustrations and data on a poster, so that they can be shared with others.

Make a simple fabric doll with a few basic garments which a child can get on and off easily. Stick to oblong shapes for the body and limbs, stuff them separately and then sew them together. Make the head attractive with plenty of woollen hair and a painted or sewn-on face. Elastic and Velcro will mean a small child can take this doll's loose trousers, skirts, T-shirt, or cape off easily.

Look in a children's clothes catalogue, list what you would expect to provide for a layette (collection of first clothes) for a new baby and then work out how much this would cost. How might parents try to be more economical?

Children's clothes are very likely to get a variety of marks and stains on them. What sort of stains are these most likely to be? Look in the shops at cleaning agents, ask other people, and look up in books to find a variety of ways of treating some of these stains. If you are able to, try out some of these methods. (It is normally easier to remove a stain as soon as it happens and it is often a good idea to try out the method of stain removal on a part of the garment which will not be seen first. This is because some methods might damage the colour or texture of the fabric.) Prepare an information sheet including some of your experimental examples and your conclusions. It would be sensible to avoid getting these cleaning agents near a baby's skin.

Carry out a survey, either in catalogues or in children's clothes shops, on children's winter coats. What important factors are you going to consider? How are you going to present your findings? Who might be interested in the information you gather?

Now that you know and understand a great deal about children's clothes set up a "Togs for Toddlers" competition. Who can design a really suitable garment for a toddler? What important points are you going to concentrate on? Before you start limit yourselves to a reasonable length of time and money. Can you ask the parent of a toddler to be the judge?

SEE ALSO

Babies to understand more about the pressures on new parents. *Playing* to find out more about why dressing up is important for young children.

See the books *Textiles for People* and *Home and Consumer* (in this series) for more information about labelling clothes.

If you are especially interested in the care of children's clothes write to Bio-tex for their leaflet (address on page 175).

Disability and handicap

Send for "Let's Get it Straight" from Mencap (address on page 180).
Write to your Community Health Council (see page 174) to find out about the details of provision for the disabled in your area. Ask particularly if there is a local Physically Handicapped and Able-Bodied club where able-bodied and disabled teenagers can join in activities together.
Write to your local Social Security Office for leaflets explaining the latest in financial benefits available.
Send for the chart "Benefits for Kids" from the Spastics Society (address on page 180).
Send for a booklet called "Abilities and Disabilities" from RADAR (address on page 179).

Ability and disability

Everyone has special abilities. What are you good at? Are there some things you wish you could do but which you are not able to do?

When we have a choice most of us like to display those things we are good at; but does everyone always have a choice? Have you ever been temporarily disabled by an accident or an illness? How did you feel about your disability? How did others react? What do you think you would have felt like if you had been told that the disability was going to be permanent?

Meeting disabled people

We all have some sort of disability in that we are not as able as we need or want to be in some situations. This sort of thing is not usually a handicap, though.

One person in ten has some more major sort of disability and one family in four has a disabled person in it. Therefore it is highly likely that we will all have the chance to meet disabled people in our families, at school, at work, on public transport, out shopping, at the cinema, or in a club.

Have you ever felt a little awkward when meeting a disabled person for the first time? Why do you think this is?

Why be well-informed?

Research has shown that children and others with disabilities do want to talk about them and they want to be as well-informed as possible.

For everyone else it can be tempting to try and avoid people with disabilities, but this is a hurtful attitude to the people with disabilities which normally comes out of embarrassment, ignorance, and fear. Make sure you know a lot about this Topic because there is so much that can be done to help, and the more well-informed you are the better you will be able to cope.

Some disabilities can be prevented by taking action, such as immunising against rubella (German measles), providing information to future parents who have a special need to know about the probable health of their baby, and by ensuring the best care of mother and baby during pregnancy and birth.

Other disabilities, such as heart defects, can sometimes be treated. There is also a great deal of work going on now to lessen the effect of some disabilities by providing early stimulation and specialised training. And there are modern drugs which can be used to control some disabilities.

Mechanical aids can make some physically disabled people's lives easier, and the use of special aids can help deaf children.

We can all also help to lessen a disability or mental handicap by the way we react to it.

What causes disability?

This is a difficult question to answer.

Disability can arise from an illness or from a motor bike, sport, or other type of accident. However, sometimes a baby is born disabled. This is something that can just happen. It need not be anybody's fault. If we look in detail at two types of disability we will see that this is true, but that there is also a great deal which can be done to help.

Mental handicap is the most common disability in this country and there are many causes. The commonest is Down's syndrome (figure 24, over the page). This is caused by an accident which happens at about the time the child is conceived. There are tiny structures found in every cell in our body which carry the messages that decide the characteristics parents will pass on to a child such as height, sex, etc. These structures are called *chromosomes*. There are twenty-three matching pairs of chromosomes in each cell, but somebody with Down's syndrome has an extra chromosome in the twenty-first pair.

It is possible to spot this during pregnancy by a process called *amniocentesis*. This is when some of the amniotic fluid which surrounds the baby in the womb is sampled. This would be done if there were a family history of handicap, or if the mother were over thirty-five, because mothers of this age are at more risk of having a Down's syndrome child. The cells in this sample are then grown for two weeks and examined to see if there are any abnormal chromosomes. This test is carried out when the mother is 14–16 weeks pregnant, and so the

Figure 24 A happy Down's syndrome child.

earliest the results would be available and an abortion might even be considered is when the foetus is eighteen weeks old. There is a small risk with amniocentesis and some people feel that they would rather not know the results anyway because it is not up to them to decide if a baby should live.

There is no absolutely right or wrong answer to this difficulty, but your opinion will be influenced by what you know and the relevant experiences you have had. What chances to find out and what sort of experiences have you and others had which might have affected the way you think about the issue of abortion?

Children with Down's syndrome are short and relatively overweight. They have distinctive facial features and large tongues which make speech difficult. They tend to be mentally slow, but although their condition cannot be put right medically a great deal can be done in the way of teaching to make the handicap less severe. They do not normally live as long as other people but there are couples who choose to adopt Down's syndrome children because they are so loving and happy.

Children who have cerebral palsy (who are spastic) are born with perfect bodies but that part of the brain which controls their movements is damaged (figure 25). This can sometimes happen because the baby was born too early, or because the mother had rubella while pregnant, or because the baby did not receive enough

Figure 25 A boy who has cerebral palsy enjoying himself.

oxygen during the birth process. So it could sometimes be prevented. However, we do not yet know all the causes of cerebral palsy. More research is urgently needed: this requires money. The sometimes odd movements of a spastic person must not lead us into thinking that they are not as bright or capable of understanding as us, or that they have different feelings.

Disabilities caused by environmental factors

The health and environment of both the prospective parents is important to the healthy development of every new baby. Smoking, drinking alcohol, and taking unprescribed drugs are particularly dangerous for the unborn child. There have been several sad cases where a baby has been born addicted to a drug. Sexually transmitted infections can also result in babies being born disabled.

The food that a pregnant woman eats and that a baby has during its first few years of life are also vitally important to the healthy formation of both the mind and body.

Children are also known to be more likely to have eczema (a severe irritation of the skin) if their parents have had it, but it is made worse by environmental causes such as certain foods, soap, heat, wool, and animals. Its severity can vary from temporary mild baby eczema to a permanently disfiguring condition which leaves the sufferer's skin sore, itchy, dry, and cracked. There are diets and creams which help.

There is also evidence to show that environmental factors such as the amount of lead or radioactivity in the atmosphere might affect the healthy development of babies in the womb and of young children.

For some of these disabilities it is interesting to reflect on why, however good the evidence, people still seem reluctant to act on it. Perhaps there are other pressures on them pushing them to act in another way? For example, why do some pregnant women still smoke even though there is overwhelming evidence to show that this leads to a baby with an unhealthily low birth weight? Why are young children taught in classrooms next to main roads while cars still emit lead fumes?

Can you think of any other examples of people acting contrary to the way the evidence suggests they should, perhaps in relation to the food they eat or the excercise they take?

Inherited disabilities

Just like we inherit brown eyes or the shape of our ear lobes from our parents, we can also inherit a disability. If a couple were worried about this they could go to a doctor for advice and information about what the risks are for them. For instance a couple might worry if another member of the family had been born disabled.

Cystic fibrosis is an example of a disability which can be inherited by a child from its parents. The parents might not be aware of the risk, however, because they could both be carriers without actually having the disease themselves. This disease chiefly affects the lungs and the digestive system. Physiotherapy to help the child to cough and clear the lungs, antibiotics to prevent infection, diet to help with digestion, and regular spells in hospital to help with the management of the disease can all help.

Another example of a disease which can be inherited is phenylketonuria (say feenile-keton-youria), which can lead to brain damage. But, as you can see in the Topic *Health and illness*, all babies are now given a blood test which can establish within a few days of birth if they have inherited this condition. A special diet can then be given if necessary.

Haemophilia (say heemo-fillia) is a special sort of inherited disability because only men suffer from it but women pass it on to the next generation. This disease affects the blood's ability to clot.

Difficulties

Some of the difficulties with disability are the ways in which we keep people who are disabled separated away, how little society helps, how ignorant most people are about how to help, and how nervous we are about our own ability to cope. Colour pictures 9 and 10 (between pages

72 and 73) show how some able-bodied people have been tackling some of the difficulties.

It is strong, sensitive, well-informed people who cope well when they meet disabled people. Do not expect this of yourself immediately. Take every opportunity you are offered to get better at being able to care for others, disabled or not. Try to treat everyone as an individual with their own special strengths and weaknesses. Your reactions to a person's disability are what will make the crucial difference between it being a difficulty or an overwhelming problem.

The quality of a person's life is very important, and part of this is having something to offer to others. What might a disabled person have to offer you?

The physical and emotional demands of coping with and caring for a disabled child within a family can be great (figure 26). There can be enormous rewards, but the parents might feel guilty about their child's disability and put a large amount of time and energy into looking after that child. This might eventually lead to illness and tensions within the family. There can also be financial difficulties if, for example, the parents are unable to go out to work because the child needs caring for or if the buildings and furniture have to be specially adapted. The

Figure 26 *Every member of this family needs caring for.*

adults may also need additional help in the home to help them cope with the everyday problems and special needs of their child and to give them a break. The child might also have to go to hospital regularly, or need a special diet, special treatment, or medicines, and all of this will take extra time and effort. Those families who do cope well are very special and greatly to be admired.

How might neighbours, relatives, and friends help a family cope with a disabled child?

What differences might it make to a youngster to have a disabled brother or sister?

Does society help enough?

We pool our resources a great deal to provide ourselves with things we could not otherwise have such as hospitals, roads, trained teachers, and some houses. Do you think we get together enough to help the disabled and handicapped? What things should society help with and how should it help?

There are also many voluntary organisations which offer support to specific groups of disabled. Where should these fit into the pattern of help offered by society? Is the best help always the most expensive?

In Great Britain, the State provides some financial help to cover

Figure 27 I use a wheelchair.

things like the cost of home adaptations and the cost of providing constant care and special transport. You can find out about the details of this provision from your local Department of Health and Social Security or Citizens Advice Bureau.

Every child is entitled to education and the 1981 Education Act recommended that whenever possible children with special needs should be educated within our ordinary primary and secondary schools (figure 27). What do you think the advantages of this might be to the child with special needs and to the other children in the school?

Children who have epilepsy used to have to go to special schools. Epilepsy means that the person has a tendency sometimes to have a seizure or fit. This can be so mild as to look like a day-dream or the person may become rigid, red in the face, and fall down unconscious with jerky movements. This happens because there is a chemical imbalance which interferes with the sending of messages to and from the brain. After a fit the person will be tired and may be confused. Most children who suffer from epilepsy attend normal schools now, and their classmates can do a great deal to help them by not making a fuss but by learning how to cope when they are needed. The person who has the fit feels no pain and will probably not remember anything about the fit at all. It is up to the people around them to check they do not hurt themselves, and to reassure them as they begin to feel better, and to give them time to recover afterwards.

There are still special schools for those children whose needs are too specialised for the ordinary education system to be able to meet them. The general advantages of these schools are that they have specially trained teachers and care assistants and good support from occupational therapists, physiotherapists, and speech therapists. They will also have much smaller classes, special equipment, and specially designed buildings. However, the children might have to travel quite a long way to their school and they will tend to be cut off from other children.

Opportunities

We all need to be given opportunities to make the most of our abilities. We also all want to be as independent as we can. This applies to disabled people as much as to able-bodied people. Anyone would get frustrated and depressed if they were not allowed to have a go at things they wanted to do. Sometimes it is tempting to be too protective of someone who is disabled, but this prevents them from experiencing new things and from gaining in confidence and ability.

There are opportunity playgroups and playgrounds where normal and disabled children can play together (figure 28, over the page).

The National Toy Libraries Association (address on page 179) lends toys to both able-bodied and disabled children and also organises research into the design and production of special toys.

Figure 28 Doing things together.

Figure 29 This toy is especially suitable for handicapped children.

Now try these

Carry out an investigation into several toys which you think might be manageable for a child with a physical disability which makes it difficult for them to grasp objects, or try to design a simple game to help some disabled children become more aware of the feel or the smell of the things around them. Figure 29 shows some examples of successful toys and activities to help you.

Disabled and handicapped people have as much right as anyone else to lead a fulfilled, happy, and independent life.

What sort of things do they need to help them to do this? How can you help?

Read the section on Down's syndrome (page 55) and then act out the parts of the parents, the social worker, and the judge from the headline in figure 30.

Down's syndrome child allowed to live against parents' wishes

Figure 30

Every Sunday morning at our local swimming pool the general public leave the water by 11 o'clock so that a club for the disabled can use the pool.

What difficulties might a boy who is very hard of hearing have at your school?

Why do you think it is important that people become well-informed about disability and handicap?

What do you think are the advantages and disadvantages of this?

What can we now do to prevent some disabilities?

64 *Disability and handicap*

Figure 31 Have you seen this sign?

Vehicles displaying this orange badge (figure 31) can often park without charge and have special places in car parks reserved for them. Can you see any examples near you? What help do you think this is?

Figure 32 Where would you expect to see this sign?

Shops displaying this sticker (figure 32) are prepared to help people who are deaf or hard of hearing. So not all good ideas cost a lot of money. Can you invent any other good ideas to help the disabled and the handicapped?

You have learned a lot about disability and handicap in this Topic. Now try and have some real contact with a disabled or handicapped person. You will be nervous but you will find parents, teachers in special schools, and people who run clubs for the disabled very welcoming and understanding.

Can you make contact with the children at your local special school?

Disability and handicap 65

> By promoting opportunities for the physically handicapped and able-bodied to come together on equal terms the barriers of fear, ignorance, and prejudice can be destroyed.

Choose one sort of disability or handicap which particularly interests you and find out more about it. You could choose to study one not mentioned in this Topic. Is there a self-help group for the disability you have chosen? Do children with this disability attend normal or special schools? Is any government help given to people with this disability?

Can you suggest a number of activities the able-bodied and physically disabled would enjoy being given the opportunity to do together at a Physically Handicapped and Able-Bodied club?

SEE ALSO

Health and illness for more information about health.
Facts of life for more information about inherited characteristics and abortion.

Books such as *If you knew Nicky* (Angus & Robertson, 1983), by Peare M. Wilson and Sandra Irvine, and *My mind is not in a wheelchair* (Hertfordshire Library Service, 1983) by Grace Hallworth, will help you to increase your awareness, knowledge, and understanding of disability.

Your local library will be able to tell you more about organisations for the disabled and handicapped in your area.

The Cystic Fibrosis Research Trust (address on page 176) provides information about how cystic fibrosis is inherited.

Diseases and immunisation

Send for information from Oxfam and UNICEF (addresses on pages 179 and 180). The National Rubella Council (address on page 179) also have a video and information pack on the special dangers of rubella.
Write to your district Health Education/Promotion Unit (address on page 174) for a variety of leaflets explaining some of the important facts about serious diseases and immunisation.

Protection against disease

Do you know which vaccinations you have had?

While babies are in the womb they are protected by the mother (as in figure 33).

While babies have their mother's antibodies they cannot make their own so immunisation does not start until the children are about three months old.

In each dose of a vaccine there is a small amount of the weakened disease. This makes the body produce its own protection against the disease but does not make the children ill. Occasionally the children will still get the infectious disease but they will not be seriously ill.

The immunisation programme

A great deal of trouble is taken to inform parents about the immunisation programme in Great Britain, and to encourage and remind them to take their children to the clinic. Leaflets and posters are on show in many places. Health visitors and doctors remind parents and in some local authorities the information is put onto a computer which issues postcards to tell parents when their clinic appointments are.

The benefits of immunisation

Why do you think it is so important that **every** child has these immunisations? Try to think of the benefits to the child, to other children, and to the rest of society. Imagine what might happen if immunisation were no longer available or if only some children were immunised.

You have probably heard or read that some vaccines have side effects. Most of these are not serious but the whooping cough vaccine

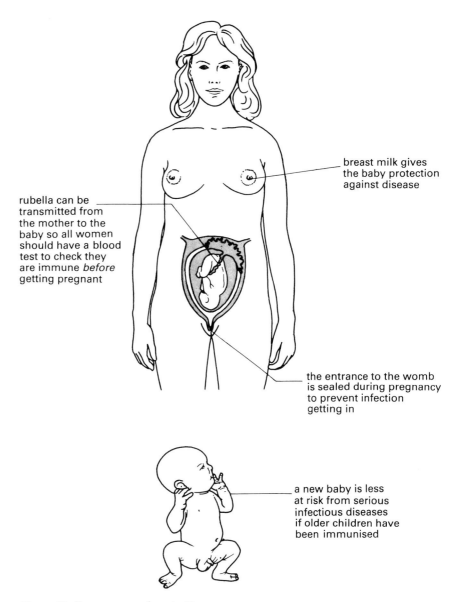

Figure 33 *Four means of protection.*

used at the time of writing can cause brain damage in an extremely small number of children. Now that you are clear about the benefits of immunisation would you recommend parents to have their children vaccinated?

Girls, girls, girls

Rubella, commonly known as German measles, is a mild infectious disease which can produce a slight rash. There is no danger to the

68   *Diseases and immunisation*

Is LIFE this cheap?

Nearly ½ million children worldwide under five contract polio every year. Polio vaccine costs about *fivepence*.

Every six seconds a child is killed and another disabled by a disease *for which immunisation exists*.

... the main causes of infant death in Birmingham 100 years ago were very much the same as in the developing world **now** – diarrhoeal diseases, malnutrition, respiratory infections and whooping cough – all symptoms of poverty.

Fighting in El Salvador stops for children's jabs

For three separate days during the next three months, the war in El Salvador is expected to cease.

Instead, the fighting will be halted to allow the United Nations Children's Fund, UNICEF, to embark on one of the most ambitious health programmes of its history.

On 3 February, 3 March and 21 April, UNICEF teams, backed by thousands of volunteers, will move across El Salvador to vaccinate every child in the country under the age of three.

Figure 34 Quotes from Oxfam and UNICEF leaflets; the article on the right is from the Observer, 23 April 1985.

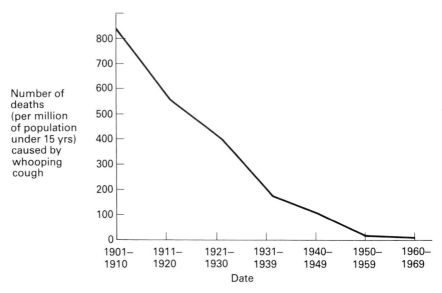

Figure 35

patient but if a woman catches rubella while she is pregnant her baby may be born with serious damage to his or her sight, hearing, heart, or brain. The vaccine has only been available since 1970 so it is not as widely understood as the other parts of the vaccination programme. It is a very safe vaccine. It can be difficult to know for certain that a girl has had rubella and made her own immunity. This vaccine is therefore offered to all teenage girls at school. It is very important that a woman does not become pregnant within three months of this immunisation. Any woman who is unsure if she is immune to this disease and who is considering becoming pregnant should have a blood test.

The challenge

In 1986 it cost only £5 to protect a child for life against the six most common and dangerous childhood diseases. Yet in 1986 fewer than 18 per cent of the developing world's children were protected (figure 34).

What does the graph in figure 35 tell you?

Can you put the information in figure 36 into your own words?

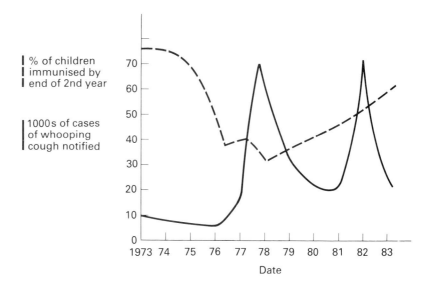

Now try these

In Great Britain, not all children have all their immunisations. Can you suggest several reasons for this?

Explain why immunisation is so important and yet so difficult in other parts of the world.

Immunisation injections do hurt. How would you cope with this difficulty when taking a small child to be immunised?

What do you think are the main advantages of immunising all children against serious infectious diseases in Great Britain?

Explain how babies in the womb and new born babies are protected from infectious disease.

Using the Health Education/Promotion Unit leaflets you sent for, plan an advertisement showing adults why all children should be immunised. What sort of approach do you think will be most effective? Are you going to try to scare them into acting sensibly or are you going to present some of the evidence in a way that will attract attention?

Using the Health Education/Promotion Unit leaflets make a chart showing some of the important facts about each disease.

In Great Britain only girls are immunised against rubella. Why do you think this is so? What might be the advantages and disadvantages of immunising boys as well?

In some countries children are not allowed to start school until their vaccination certificates have been seen. What do you think about this system?

It would be interesting to find out how much knowledge other people your age have about this important Topic. Do all the girls in your school have their rubella immunisation? Do they know why it is important?

SEE ALSO

Health and illness for more information about less serious illnesses and how to look after children who are ill. *Children have rights* is about the right of children worldwide to be protected from disease.

Some of you might be able to visit a clinic and report back about how the immunisations were carried out and how the children and parents felt.

Experts

 Collect several "problem pages" from magazines, and a selection of books, leaflets, and articles which give advice to parents about how to bring up young children.

Important experts on children

Can you think of any decisions you have made where you have used an expert's advice? Perhaps you have been on a special diet, bought an expensive item, or learned a new skill. Was the expert's advice helpful? Look at the family in figure 37 and then try to write a list of all the experts they might be involved with.

Figure 37 *We all need expert advice at some time.*

Pictures 1 and 2
What have these libraries done to make books interesting to children? Are your local libraries friendly and attractive places to go to?

Picture 3
Chinese New Year is an important and colourful public celebration.

Pictures 4 and 5
This is Richard's bedroom. He is 15 months old. What sort of things have been done to make the room bright and interesting without spending too much money?

Pictures 6 and 7
These two bedrooms belong to Ian and Kevin, and to Catherine. How have they been designed so as to:
1 make best use of the space available
2 be flexible
3 be appealing to young children and easy for them to use?

Picture 8
This jumper is made by knitting simple rectangles. One dress is made from a single pattern piece and the other is made from a kit.

Pictures 9 and 10
Doing things together can mean that everybody enjoys the activity more.

Did you include any of the following?

General Practitioners (GPs) provide everyday medical care and emergency medical care. It is also part of their job to help you to use the other areas of the health service such as a hospital specialist. Has anyone in your class been referred to a specialist?

GPs often hold clinics outside normal surgery hours for things such as vaccinations and antenatal care.

In order to get the best out of your GP try to be clear about what you want to say or ask, and when you are making an appointment with the receptionist say how urgent the problem is. What sort of things could make this quite difficult to do?

School doctors do not usually provide treatment. If they notice anything wrong when they are carrying out school medicals they write either to your GP or to a hospital specialist. All children have a school medical examination when they start school.

What sort of important things do you think should be checked at this medical examination?

Nurses such as the district nurse work in the community alongside the GP. Some doctors have their own nurse working in the surgery. School nurses are responsible for promoting health education in a number of schools.

The other type of nurse many families come into contact with is the *midwife*. These nurses specialise in the care of pregnant women, the birth of babies, and their care until they are ten days old. All midwives have a basic nurse training and a specialist qualification too. Some work in hospitals while others work within the community with the GPs. Often there are also specially trained children's nurses in hospital.

Health visitors are also qualified nurses who have followed an additional period of training. They specialise in looking after the very young and the very old. They advise on the prevention of disease and carry out some of the developmental checks on young children. They visit people in their homes and also work with GPs in their surgeries. Parents often meet their health visitor at the well-baby clinic when they take their baby to be weighed, and they can ask about small things which might be worrying them then.

Why is it so important to try to *prevent* disease and ill health?

Hospital specialists such as *obstetricians*, who look after pregnant women and their babies, and *paediatricians*, who look after children, and *ophthalmologists*, who specialise in the treatment of eye problems, can be contacted when necessary through your GP.

Dietitians are also available to advise on what we should normally eat to stay healthy and what we should eat under special circumstances such as pregnancy, or while we are very young or old or if we are ill.

Social workers are responsible for organising facilities for the care of the elderly, the handicapped, and the needy. They supervise day nurseries, license childminders, and provide support for families who have difficulty in coping.

This sort of provision can vary from area to area. What is available near you?

Dentists work in their own practice and they also provide treatment via the school health service. *Orthodontists* specialise in straightening crooked teeth.

What sort of things can be done to make children's visits to the dentist go smoothly?

Playgroup leaders and *nursery school teachers* are often consulted by parents for advice. They are seen regularly by parents in an informal way and there are plenty of opportunities to talk about something that is worrying them.

Grandparents and *other parents* are also often asked for advice. Parents sometimes get together to help each other, as when organising a speaker for an evening talk through the playgroup, or through organisations such as Gingerbread (address on page 177) where single parents help each other.

Marriage guidance counsellors and *child guidance clinics* can also offer expert advice to parents.

Some of the above people are experts mainly because of their training. Some of them have had no training but they have had a great deal of experience.

Now go back and reread the descriptions of some of the experts who are important to families. Have some of them had more training than others? Have some of them had a great deal of experience?

How do experts make sure they keep up to date?

Experts who disagree

Read these two expert opinions about nappies:

"I always use disposable nappies because although they are quite expensive they are so hygienic and convenient. I recommend changing a baby very often to avoid nappy rash."

"My daughter has towelling nappies and rubber pants because I find they save me from having to change her quite so often. They are also cheaper. I always put a thick layer of waterproof cream on her bottom to stop it getting sore."

What do these two people disagree about? Try to think of several reasons which might explain why they hold these different views.

Figure 38

Say what the disagreements are between the people in figure 38. What else would the parents of a young child have to consider before they made up their own minds about this matter?

There are several other areas where expert opinion is divided. Using a variety of books which offer advice on bringing up children look up what they say on subjects such as "leaving a child to cry", "feeding by the clock", and "introducing mixed feeding". Ask some parents, grandparents, and a health visitor what they think about these issues. Do they all agree?

What can you do when the experts do not agree? Getting expert advice does not rid you of the responsibility for making your own decisions, but it will usually help you make a better decision.

Experts make their minds up when they have seen some evidence. It sometimes helps to ask what that evidence was, for instance "What makes you think that?" If you are reading a book written by an expert you can look and see what training or experience they have had. This will help you decide where they might have obtained the evidence their advice is based on.

Look at the books, articles, and leaflets you collected. Can you find out what sort of training or experience the authors have had? Does this information alter your opinion about their advice? Are any of these experts being paid to encourage you to take a particular course of action?

Now try these

People are often tense and worried when they go to an expert. Why do you think this is?

Act out two parents talking to the doctor about what they should do when their child cries and cries when put to bed at night. They find this upsetting and annoying and are frightened at what they might do to the child if this continues. Try to imagine what the parents and the doctor would really feel like in this situation. Do you think the parents would say what was worrying them straight away?

When you have done this course you are probably going to be consulted by some people for your considered opinion. They will expect you to be able to give them good information. What could you say and do if you are unsure of the answer to their question?

> Take my word for it, it worked for all my children. I have never known it to fail.

> You could try, I do not guarantee it will work but I do not think it will do any harm to try.

Which of these two pieces of advice would you be more likely to take and why?

Look at the magazine problem pages you collected. Can you find any examples of the expert trying to reassure and calm the writers of the letters? Can you find any places where the evidence behind the opinion is given, or where the reader is referred to another expert person or publication? Can you spot anything which tells you why the person giving the advice is thought suitable to give it?

Think of a real decision which might have to be taken in a family, and collect as many different points of view about it as you can. You could invite some parents to come and discuss the issue with you. It could, perhaps, be concerning family rules such as at what time the members of the family should be in at night, or whether they should be home for mealtimes. Or, it might be a decision related to who does which jobs around the home.

SEE ALSO

Feelings and behaviour
Health and illness } to start to become an expert yourself!

You could invite the school health visitor to tell you about school medicals, or an expert in one area to come to talk to you about their work. What difficulties do they have when offering expert advice?

Facts of life

Write to your district Health Education/Promotion Unit for factual information about sex, conception, contraception, pregnancy, birth and sexually transmitted infections.
Write to The Society for the Protection of the Unborn Child (address on page 180) for a copy of "Human Concern".
Write to Johnson and Johnson (address on page 177) for a booklet which explains the changes which take place in all of us during adolescence.

Ways of learning

Most adults seem to find it difficult to talk to young people about the facts of both life and death. Why do you think this is so?

Adults also sometimes disagree with each other about what, when, and how much young people should be told about these. Can you find out what some of these disagreements are about?

Why do you think some adults feel that it is very important you are well-informed, while others think that ignorance is no bad thing? Why do some adults think it important you are encouraged to hold a certain point of view while others think you should be told about several different points of view?

Discuss, in small groups, how much you think people two years younger than you should be told, about sexual matters and then discuss how much knowledge should be made freely available to you.

There are many different ways of learning, and what we find out in school is only a very small part of our total knowledge.

Write down a list of all the different ways in which 12-year-olds might have learned about the facts of life and sex. Where and from whom do children learn about this?

Do you think some of these ways of learning are better than others Why? What sort of wrong information might they have learned? Do you think the adults in charge of these 12-year-olds could have helped to make this learning easier and better? How?

Might some 12-year-olds be worried about anything they have heard or seen? Where could they go or whom could they ask to find out the truth and be reassured?

Get together with a friend and discuss the ways in which you learned what you know about sex and the facts of life. Can you spot any gaps or slants in your own education about sex?

Because this is not a subject which is openly discussed "old wives'

Figure 39 We all have different needs.

tales" tend to be believed. How many of these can you collect?

What sort of things to do with sexual matters might the people in figure 39 need to find out or want to discuss? How could they do this? What difficulties might they come across?

Can you believe your own eyes?

It is very difficult to get an honest and accurate picture of what other people around us are really doing and feeling. Look quickly at figure 40 (over the page) and then describe what you saw to a friend.

Now look at the picture again. What did you notice? What did you fail to see? Did you jump to any assumptions? Did your friends or

Figure 40 What could be happening here?

Figure 41

perhaps your teacher "read" the picture at all differently? In how many different ways could this picture be read?

Try out a small experiment for yourselves. Estimate what percentage of people in a large group you are familiar with (such as your year group at school, a club, team, or workforce) smoke. Now ask each one to tell you honestly whether they do or not. What was the result? Did you over or under "guesstimate"? You might find it difficult to get at the truth because the people might boast to you or be unwilling to give

an honest answer; if the group is very large you could check your answer by asking just a representative sample.

We all need to be aware that what we see around us will affect our own decisons. However, do we always see and hear the true situation (figure 41)?

Changing

In how many different ways have the people in figure 42 changed as they have got older? Try to include the sort of changes you cannot actually see as well as the more obvious ones. Can you organise these changes into groups?

During the time we are in the top of the primary school and then in secondary school we change very fast in a large number of different ways. This is called *adolescence*. We start to move from childhood to adulthood. A lot of these changes are to do with our bodies gradually becoming capable of reproduction.

Figure 42 Growing, changing, developing.

Three things that concern teenagers about adolescence

Adolescence can leave us feeling unsettled because our bodies start to do some quite surprising things!

As boys begin to grow up most of them will have erections. The penis will become stiff and a small amount of liquid containing a large number of sperm will spurt out of the end of the penis. This can happen when the boy is asleep (a "wet dream"), and also during the day. A mature male's reproductive system is continually making sperm and this is a harmless and pleasurable way of releasing them, but it can sometimes be awkward.

A "period" is when the girl's body prepares a clean, healthy place for the baby that could be conceived that month to start its life. A girl's first periods are likely to be small and irregular. All through her reproductive life emotional upset, severe illness, or drastic loss of weight may cause these periods to stop. Roughly every month the lining of the womb and, when her periods are regular, the unfertilised egg are discarded with a small quantity of blood. Girls use sanitary towels or tampons to protect them during these 3–7 days. Exercise, hair washing, and baths will all help the girl feel better during this time. (It only takes a very small amount of blood to colour a large amount of water, so although a girl might feel she is losing a lot of blood if, for example, a little leaks into the bath water, this is very unlikely to be the case.) At around the age of 45–50 (but it may be earlier or later) a woman's periods will gradually stop, and she will no longer be capable of having a baby. This is called the *menopause*.

You might have heard that some women experience *pre-menstrual tension* (PMT). This is a feeling of discomfort, depression, or bad temper before or during their periods. This happens because their monthly cycle is controlled by chemicals in the bloodstream. The chemical hormones oestrogen and progesterone vary in amount throughout the month. The changes in the levels of these hormones can cause some women problems, and this is something fewer women are prepared to put up with nowadays. Exercises, mild pain killers, and, in extreme cases, hormone treatment from the doctor can all help.

Young children often discover that it feels nice to touch or rub their private parts or sexual organs. This is harmless, and does not mean the child is going to be over concerned with sex when older. In teenagers this masturbation is a private and enjoyable way of releasing sexual tension. It will not cause any damage at all and is probably best ignored by adults.

Suitable behaviour

Should any of the changes described above affect the way in which we behave? Is it okay for small girls and boys to play on the beach with no clothes on, to have baths together, to hold hands with other girls and boys, to leave the door open when they go to the toilet, and to see each other getting dressed? Are these things as acceptable for adults to do?

Can you think of any other ways in which this development, that takes place in each of us, also alters the ways in which we behave, particularly where members of the opposite sex are concerned?

What do you think the reasons might be for these changes in

behaviour? Young adults have a powerful sex drive. This is nature's way of making sure that most of them will want to have babies and so continue a healthy race of human beings. Is it suitable for this sex drive to be allowed uncontrolled freedom? Why is it important to control it?

Usually this sexual attraction is for members of the opposite sex, but some teenagers may find that they are attracted to members of the same sex and this may or may not last. Homosexuality amongst adults is not against the law but individuals might need time and help to adjust to this knowledge about themselves. To whom might a young person go if they wanted to discuss this matter privately? What support is there for homosexuals in our society?

Teenagers become capable of sex long before they are able or willing to cope with the consequences. What might these "consequences" be? How does society discourage young people from sexual activity?

In small groups try to complete each of these sentences several times.

"Sex is right when . . ."
"Sex is wrong when . . ."

The answers you have given will be personal ones based on your knowledge and beliefs. Remember, someone else with more or less knowledge or different beliefs might give a different answer.

Conception

In a long-term relationship, such as marriage, many couples want to have children.

What sort of things make couples want to or not want to have children? Try to think of several reasons and then group them under headings such as financial, medical, etc.

Are couples really free to choose to or to choose not to have children? Do you think there might be any pressure on them? From where might this pressure come?

There is a self-support group for couples who have chosen to be childless. Why do you think they feel the need for this mutual support?

In some countries there is much more pressure on couples than there is in Great Britain. In China there are financial incentives and liberal abortion laws to encourage couples to have only one child, whilst in Romania there are financial penalties against the childless and abortion is illegal in most circumstances. Clearly the birth of babies is important to the State as well as to individual couples.

Inheritance

At the moment of conception decisions are made about what a new baby will inherit from both its parents. Inherited factors include our height, bone structure, ear shape, skin, hair and eye colour, and the shape of our mouth, nose, and forehead. We cannot choose what we will inherit and only identical twins inherit exactly the same things. However, even they do not stay identical in many ways for long because their environment causes each of them to develop differently.

The instructions regarding these inherited factors are in chromosomes and we all have twenty-three pairs of chromosomes in all our body cells. Mature reproductive cells, eggs and sperms, have twenty-three single chromosomes (not pairs). So when an egg and a sperm join at conception the fertilised ovum has its own special pattern of twenty-three pairs, half from the mother and half from the father. Different eggs or sperm from the same person contain some different instructions, so children from the same parents will all be different from each other in some ways (except identical twins).

Contraception

This is a subject which is rather more freely discussed than it used to be. It is quite common to see newspaper and magazine articles on this subject and some contraceptives are displayed attractively in most chemists.

Contraceptives are considered necessary by many people because they do not want to start a baby each time they have sexual intercourse. This means that the majority of babies born can be planned for and very much wanted. Couples can choose when in their lives they will have their children and they can space them out as they wish.

Which of the people's attitudes in figure 43 seem sensible to you?

Lots of people hold very strong views about the subject of contraception. Investigate and try to explain how someone's age, religion, sex, and family upbringing might affect their attitude towards contraception.

In order for a contraceptive to be successful it must:
a) prevent the process whereby the woman's ovum is fertilised by the man's sperm and then this fertilised ovum implants itself into the lining of the woman's womb and starts to divide and grow.
It should also be:
b) easily available
c) not too expensive
d) pleasant to use
e) simple to use
f) very reliable when used correctly
g) have no serious side effects.

Using the Health Education/Promotion Unit leaflets on the various types of contraceptive investigate how far each of these achieves these seven things.

In what ways do you think contraception is important nationally and internationally?

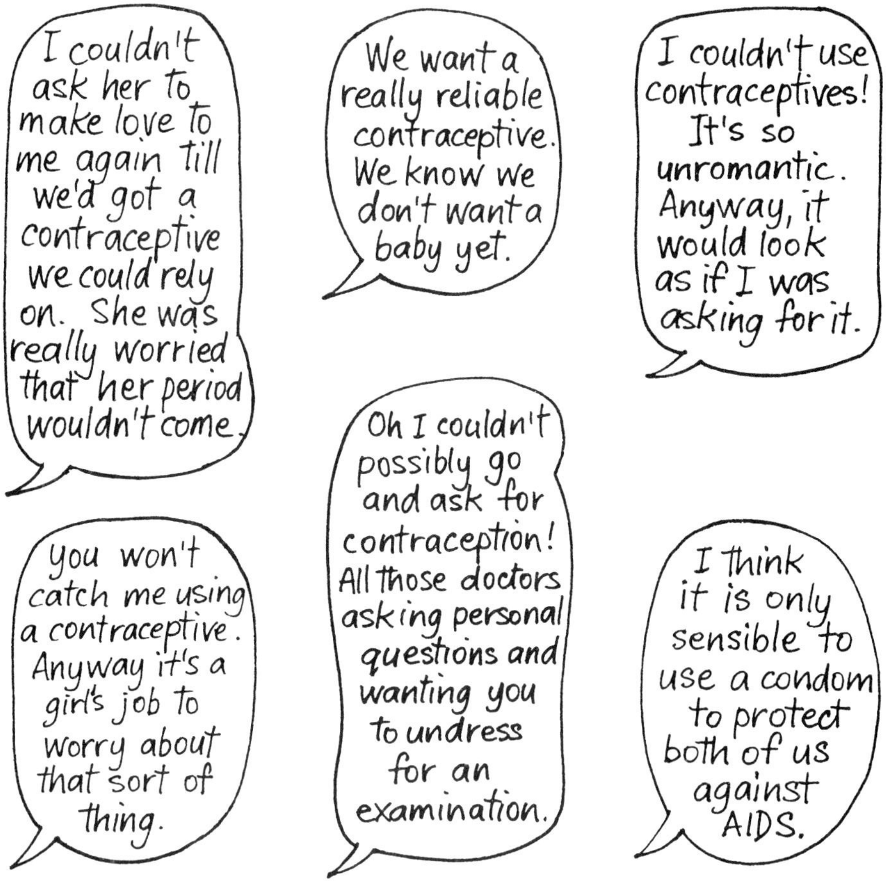

Figure 43

Speech bubbles:
- "I couldn't ask her to make love to me again till we'd got a contraceptive we could rely on. She was really worried that her period wouldn't come."
- "We want a really reliable contraceptive. We know we don't want a baby yet."
- "I couldn't use contraceptives! It's so unromantic. Anyway, it would look as if I was asking for it."
- "You won't catch me using a contraceptive. Anyway it's a girl's job to worry about that sort of thing."
- "Oh I couldn't possibly go and ask for contraception! All those doctors asking personal questions and wanting you to undress for an examination."
- "I think it is only sensible to use a condom to protect both of us against AIDS."

The three most common places to obtain contraceptives are at a chemist's shop, at a GP's surgery, at a Family Planning clinic, or at a Brook clinic. What might be the advantages and disadvantages of each of these?

Some types of contraceptive also have another advantage. There is a great deal of concern about the increasing level of sexually transmitted infections. Those methods of contraception which provide a physical barrier between the couple can help prevent the spread of these. The contraceptive which does this most effectively is the condom, used by the man.

People who have a large number of different sexual partners or who start to have sex at an early age are at particular risk of getting one of these infections.

It is very important that both partners are treated as early as possible. Most infections can be treated at a special clinic where the doctors and nurses are very used to treating sexually transmitted infections and do not feel embarrassed. People are treated confidentially and the treatment usually involves taking pills. However, because some people are reluctant to seek treatment the National Health Service has a recorded telephone message people can listen to to find out more. The number will be under "Venereal Disease" in your telephone book.

Sexually transmitted infections can cause damage to babies before and after birth. They can also cause permanent and severe damage to grown up men and women. There is considerable concern expressed about the spread of these infections today. People can only act responsibly if they are well-informed. In 1987 the government sent a leaflet about Auto Immune Deficiency Syndrome (AIDS) to every house in Great Britain, to give people some basic information about this disease.

Miscarriage and abortion

Sadly one pregnancy in about five ends before the baby is sufficiently developed to survive outside the mother's body. The most common cause of this in early pregnancy is that there is something wrong with the baby. Doctors call this a natural abortion.

Sometimes a woman might discover she is pregnant when she does not want to be. What sort of circumstances might lead to this?

It is possible, if two doctors agree, to have an abortion in Great Britain. This means that the foetus will be medically made to leave the womb before it can survive on its own. What sort of very strong reasons might cause a woman to seek an abortion?

The number of weeks into a pregnancy at which abortions are still legal is decided by parliament. As more and more advances are made in saving the lives of very premature babies this date becomes very controversial. One day a medical team may be fighting to save the life of a 22-week-old foetus, and the next day they could be carrying out an abortion on a foetus of nearly this age.

A very difficult question to ask yourself is "When do I believe life begins?" It could be at the moment of conception, or when the fertilised ovum implants in the womb, or when the embryo's nervous system starts to develop, or when the mother first feels the baby move inside her, or when the baby is born.

Whether you consider "the morning after pill", or an intra-uterine device inserted after intercourse to prevent pregnancy, to have an abortion or not will depend on when you believe life starts. (To find out more about these look at the information you sent for from the Health Education/Promotion Unit.)

Listen to what this 21-year-old girl said two and a half years after having had an abortion: "I was scared to go to the doctor's so I did not go for a few weeks. When the doctor told me I was pregnant she also told me when my baby would have been born. Now every year when that date comes round I feel sad because it could have been my child's birthday. I still think I did the right thing but it changed me forever and I will never forget it."

What other alternatives might this girl have had? Why do you think she chose an abortion?

Read the information from the Society for the Protection of the Unborn Child to help you understand one sort of viewpoint on this important issue.

Some couples choose to have a pregnancy ended because they are told by the doctors that their baby is badly handicapped.

Infertility

The most common cause of infertility in a man is a low sperm count, and in a woman it is when the tubes which carry the ova from the ovaries to the womb become blocked. Both of these conditions can be caused by a variety of things. There are several options available to infertile couples.

If it is the woman who is infertile then she might have an operation to try to unblock her Fallopian tubes. Or hormone treatment might be used to stimulate the woman to produce more ova. Or the woman's ova might be removed surgically, fertilised with her husband's sperm in a laboratory, and then once the process of division and growth has started these are carefully transferred back into the woman's womb: this is commonly known as a test-tube baby. Surrogate motherhood is when a woman's ovum is artificially fertilised by sperm from another woman's husband, and this surrogate mother then "carries" the baby until it is born, when she hands it over to the couple. This is a very controversial area of parenthood. It is illegal to sell babies for money in Great Britain.

If it is the man who is infertile then artificial insemination by donor can be used. This is when the woman's ovum is artificially fertilised with the sperm of a fertile man which has been donated anonymously for this purpose.

The start of life

Couples are often very keen to find out as soon as possible if the woman has conceived and is pregnant. Use your information from the Health Education/Promotion Unit to find out what the first signs might be. Why is it important women know they are pregnant as early as possible?

Looking after this new life

The information from the Health Education/Promotion Unit will tell you what can be done to care for the health of the pregnant woman and the baby in the womb. This is considered so important that employers are legally bound to allow pregnant women time off work to go to their ante-natal clinic appointments.

At these appointments several checks are carried out to ensure the health of the pregnant woman and her baby. The woman is weighed, her blood pressure is taken, and a sample of her urine is checked. She will also have a blood sample taken.

Now try these

At what age do you think you might settle down with a partner? Might you have children? What sort of thing will this depend on?

A large amount of money is spent on the research and development of new contraceptives. Why do you think this is so? What would you think it important to know about a new contraceptive?

Adults might vary the contraceptive they use several times throughout their lives. Suggest when and what some of these changes might be and say why you think they might occur.

In Great Britain there are many unplanned pregnancies. Why do you think this is so? What do you think the consequences might be?

Why should a woman who is trying to become pregnant:
a) not smoke
b) not take any medicines at all unless told to by the doctor
c) find out as early as possible if she is pregnant?

What sort of things could be done to encourage a pregnant woman to keep her ante-natal clinic appointments regularly?

Abortion is always wrong.

What do you think? Why do some people believe this?

The spotlight does tend to be on the woman during pregnancy but the prospective father also has important needs which should be considered.
Try to put yourself in his place and imagine what his rôle might be and what he might feel like.

SEE ALSO

Diseases and immunisation for more about rubella.

A few of you might be able to visit an ante-natal clinic and then report back to the rest of your group about what you see.

Invite a couple who are expecting a baby to come and tell you about their feelings and the preparations they are making.

Invite a health visitor to come and take your blood pressure before and after exercise. Find out why blood pressure is an indication of normal health and why raised blood pressure is dangerous in late pregnancy.

Families

Collect lots of pictures from magazines of people of different ages. Collect examples of families from television, films, and adverts. Write to the organisation "Gingerbread" (address on page 177) to find out more about families with one parent.

Today and tomorrow

Carry out a survey amongst people your own age. Taking care to act in a sensitive way, find out how many children there are in their families and how many children they imagine themselves having in the future. What does your evidence suggest about the size of families to come? Can you suggest any reasons for your results? Do they show hope for the future?

Families are all different

If you have ever lived with another family, even for just a short space of time such as a holiday, you will know that families feel very different from each other when you are inside them. There are clearly lots of different types of family.

Using the pictures of people you collected put them into different groups, each of which you think could be called "a family".

Is there anything which all your paper "families" have in common? Do they involve more than one generation, do the people live together, do they love and care for each other, do they have the same surname, do these "families" include members of each sex, do they share their money, are any of the members married, and do they rely on each other for support? Are there any other ways in which these "families" might be like each other?

Now try to say what a family is. In pairs complete the sentence "A family is . . .". Read out each statement and then discuss them.

Do you think there is such a thing as a typical family?

Families are in a constant state of change as the members grow older and become more or less dependent on each other. Using each of the following terms as many times as you like make up several possible family "life cycles".

single
adult
courtship
cohabitation

marriage
childless couple
birth of child(ren)
child(ren) grow(s) up

separation	children leave home
divorce	death of spouse
reconciliation	step-parenthood
remarriage	grandchildren
one-parenthood	great-grandchildren

Who's who?

If it is difficult to say what a typical family is like it is also difficult to say what a typical family member is like. Look at colour pictures 11–16 (between pages 136 and 137). Which of those people do you think is a grandparent?

They are all grandparents! As you can see they all view the role of grandparent very differently. What should a grandparent be like? Are there any qualities you think every grandparent should possess?

If there was a competition for "The Best Dad" what qualities would you, as a judge, be looking for?

Real families

Nowadays we all have to try to be well informed and sensitive when we think of what the word "family" means to us. We are often not helped in this by films, television, and advertisements which tend to present a rather one-sided view of family life.

Look at the example of families you collected. Do they paint an honest picture of what you know today's families are really like?

The family today

There are five major changes taking place in lots of families today:

1) As we have already seen there are more and more different sorts of family patterns.

Can we say that any one type of family structure is best at meeting the needs of all the members of a family?

2) There are more and more divorces (see figure 44, over the page).

You used to have to be wealthy to afford a divorce and it was a lengthy, unpleasant experience. This is no longer true. Alongside today's rising divorce rate there is also an increase in the number of remarriages and therefore in the number of step-families.

What sort of difficulties might step-families have to overcome? Are there any times when you think being a member of a step-family might be especially awkward?

3) More couples are living together without getting married, either because they are unable to marry, perhaps because one of them is married already, or the relationship is only intended as a short temporary one, or because they can borrow more money to buy a

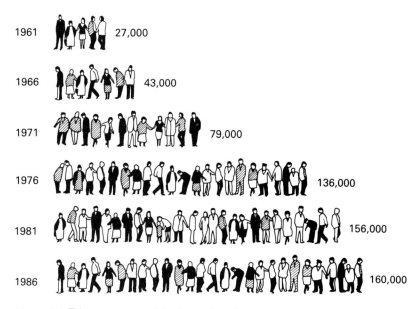

Figure 44 Divorces granted in Great Britain.

house, or it could be a sort of trial marriage. Some couples do choose to cohabit, though, rather than to get married. In fact more than half of the illegitimate births in this country are registered jointly by both parents, which suggests that although not married they are in a stable relationship.

Should a couple be married before they have children?

What does to be "illegitimate" mean? Some people think that it does unnecessary harm to use the term and that we should simply get rid of it. What do you think?

4) More families are becoming involved in looking after their elderly members. Research shows that this responsibility more often involves the women of the family. There are more old people today. More people than ever before will know both their grandparents and their great-grandparents.

What do you think might be the advantages and disadvantages of this change in the structure of the family?

5) There has been a change in the rôles people have within the family. Large numbers of women used to give up their jobs automatically when they married. Instead they set up home, and settled down to bring up their children. The man used to always be the main breadwinner.

What tends to happen now?

Till death us do part

Write down the age you expect to live to. Under this write down the age at which you see yourself settling down with someone else and

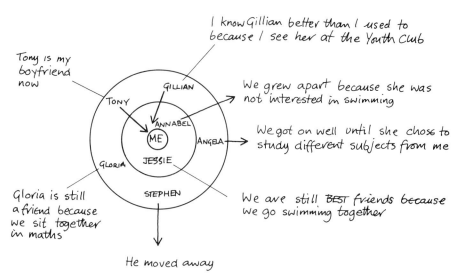

Figure 45 A friendship pattern.

perhaps marrying them. Now take the bottom figure away from the top one. What is the answer? What does this answer show?

Draw three circles on a piece of paper as shown in figure 45, and put your own name in the centre one. Now in the next circle out write the name(s) of your **best** friend(s) when you were in your last year at primary school. In the next circle out write the names of some of your other friends at this time. Do not do anything else to the names of those people with whom you have the same relationship today but put an arrow and a label on each of the other names to say how your friendship has changed and why you think this has happened.

Look at each other's "friendship patterns". Can you see any similarities or any differences in such things as number of friends, which sex they were, and how many friendships have altered over time and with changing circumstances?

You might like to do another friendship pattern for yourself today, but this might be something you wish to keep more private. When you look at it yourself though try to spot the differences in the friendships you now make.

What would you look for in a partner? Try to put your reasons in order of importance. It might be interesting for the boys and girls in your group to do this piece of work separately, and then to discuss the results with each other. Think about things like interests, reputation, money, family, habits, as well as looks and personality.

How could you tell what a friend's attitude to your family, honesty, or hard work was?

What sort of things do you think a couple should talk about before they settle down together or get married? What sort of difficulties are they likely to have if they do not talk about these things?

A great many teenage marriages end in divorce. Can you think why this is so? Can you suggest anything that might make teenage marriages more likely to succeed?

One-parent families

What are the main causes of one parent being left to manage a family single-handed? (see figure 46).

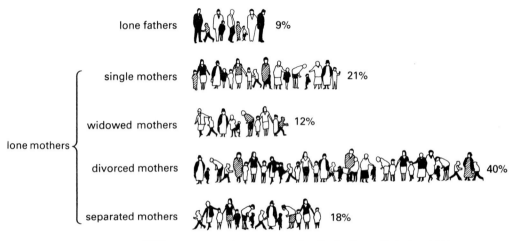

Figure 46 Different types of one-parent family in Great Britain, 1982–4.

Most divorces happen because the couple do not get on together any longer. It can be a difficult and unhappy time when a couple divorce or separate. Forty per cent of the children in these families lose touch altogether with the parent who does not have custody. They usually lose touch with other members from that side of the family as well. There can be a great deal of bitterness between the adults involved which will affect the children. Often the children hope for a long time that their parents will get back together again, and they might demand a great deal of extra attention.

What sort of things do you think a couple with young children who want to get divorced could helpfully discuss with an outside person? How might this help them to come to some agreements which will make things easier for the children?

There are numerous legal terms used to describe some of these agreements such as: access, maintenance, joint custody, and care and control. Try to find out what sort of things these terms cover. An adult who has been divorced, or a book specialising in divorce from the library will help you with this.

Today more than one in eight families with dependent children is headed by a lone parent. What do you think the main differences might be between living in a two-parent or a one-parent household?

"Gingerbread" is a national network of self-help groups for lone parents. These can help to stop the adults feeling isolated in a society where most adults go out as couples, and where they are often trying to be both a caring parent and earn a living at the same time.

Nearly a half of all lone-parent families have considerable money problems. How might this affect the children?

Family membership

There are several ways of becoming a member of a family. You can marry into it, be born into it, or be adopted into it.

Although legally very different from being fostered, adoption can follow on from the successful fostering of a child with a family or, in some cases, a step-parent might adopt a child. In Great Britain the Social Services departments of local authorities act as the legal parents of a very large number of children, some of whom will only be away from their families for a short time. However, about half of these children will be away from their families for much longer and in some cases it will be permanent.

Can you think of any reasons why children might need permanent homes and families other than the ones they were born into?

Adoption is even more binding than a wedding because a marriage can be ended by divorce but adoption is for ever. An adoption order can only be made by a court of law, and the judge must be satisfied that it would be the very best thing for the child. The consent of the child's birth-parents is usually required. An adopted child becomes a full and legitimate member of their new family.

Why might a single person or a married couple want to adopt a child?

There are many children with special needs who would like to be adopted. They are sometimes mentally handicapped, physically disabled, emotionally disturbed, or maybe they are older children with little experience of family life or groups of brothers and sisters who want to stay together.

Why do you think there are very few babies available for adoption today?

If a local authority cannot find a family for a child in its own area the British Agencies for Adoption and Fostering, which is a national organisation, can help by including details of the child in its "Be My Parent" booklet. There are roughly 380 copies of this around the country with local authorities and adoption agencies. They are shown to prospective parents. Some children will also be advertised in *The Guardian* newspaper's "Child of the Month" feature.

What else could and is being done to help these children find a family? Have you a "Homefinder shop" near you?

Some people feel that black children should only be adopted by black families and that white children should only be adopted by white families. They feel that this is very important to the child's sense of identity. Can you try to explain this point of view?

Most of the families who wish to adopt children are white. Could this be a problem for black children in care? What sort of things should be done to encourage more families from different ethnic groups to consider fostering or adopting a child?

Adopted children over eighteen years of age can obtain a copy of their original birth certificate. If they want to find their birth-parents they will be advised on the best way to go about this search and counselled on the effects this action might have on them and the people around them.

Look at a birth certificate. What sort of information is there on it? If the parents of a child are not married the father's name will usually only be on the certificate if both parents want it to be there.

In a survey carried out amongst young adults who had been adopted they said they felt it had been a happy experience. However, they also said that their feelings about being adopted had changed from time to time as they grew up.

What sort of things might have caused these changes in feelings?

Other ideas

1) **Polygamy** (the right of a person to have more than one spouse at the same time) is still popular in West Africa. Below are two quotes from men who have more than one wife.

What sort of problems do you think the first man is talking about? In what way could a man gain authority, prestige, and wealth from having more than one wife?

Historically polygamy began as a way of ensuring that large numbers of women whose husbands had been killed in a war were cared for.

2) There are **collective farms** in Israel called **kibbutzim** where adults live as married couples in their own houses but the children are all brought up by trained nurses and teachers rather than only by their parents. The children see their parents every day but the emphasis is on community rather than family life. Both tasks and money are shared amongst the adults.

What do you think might be the advantages to the children of living like this?

3) Many people believe that there are more important reasons for marrying someone other than love or physical attraction. They would put the coming together of two families as a very important part of marriage and might "arrange" a marriage between two families.

There is much less divorce when marriages start out in this way. The families regard it as very important to all the members that the couple stay together and will go to a great deal of trouble to help them.

In what ways could these families help these marriages to last?

Now try these

What sort of needs do the people in figure 47 have that their families should try to meet?

Figure 47 We all need different things from a family.

Marriage involves two families as well as two individuals joining together.

Have you ever lived with another family, even for a short space of time? Describe what it felt like. If someone comes to stay with your family what sort of preparation do you make? When a visitor is present do your family act in the same way they normally do?

How true is this? Might it cause any difficulties?

Families vary greatly in their attitudes to things such as bedtimes, mealtimes, and doing jobs around the house. Write a report saying what you have noticed about different families' attitudes to these things. You will not need to name particular families.

Why do the following need to know and understand clearly what today's families are really like: the politician, the employer, the head teacher, and the social worker? What sort of decisions do each of these make which affect the family?

It is difficult to reach a decision about whether marriage is more or less popular today. What evidence is there to support one side of this argument?

What do you think will happen to marriage in the future? What makes you think this?

Women account for forty per cent of the workforce and many men share the running of a home and the care of children. Has their upbringing prepared them well for this? Should your upbringing prepare you for this sort of thing? In what way would this be possible?

In a letter to a magazine problem page a teenager wrote: "My parents have just got divorced and I feel fed up . . . money seems to be short . . . and I can't help missing the times when we were all happy together but I don't miss the rows! I feel a bit awkward when my Dad comes to collect me . . ." What sort of thing would you write to her?

By far the most popular time for adopted children to set about finding out more about their natural parents is when they get married and have children of their own. Why do you think this is so?

Why do you think the law does not allow adopted children to try to trace their birth-parents until they are eighteen years old? Why do you think they are also advised to do this thoughtfully and carefully? There are agencies which will help trace parents. What advantages might using one of these have?

Although it is a difficult decision to make, it is a responsible and caring one.

In what ways might a parent who decides to have their child adopted be said to be acting responsibly and in a caring way?

> Family members are held together by affection for each other, shared experiences and responsibilities towards each other – not by ties of blood.

Do you agree? Either describe some important experiences you have shared with your family or describe some of the responsibilities to each other the members of your family have.

It has been predicted that the "step-family" will become the typical family. What do you think might cause this to happen?

Suggest some practical ways in which a divorcing couple can consider their children's feelings. Should the adults talk to the children about the reasons for the divorce?

Try to record an interview with a marriage guidance counsellor. Prepare your questions beforehand and speak clearly so that the rest of the group enjoy listening to it.

What might the good and bad effects of unemployment be on family life?

SEE ALSO

Babies to find out more about the joy and strain having a baby can bring to a family.

Children have rights will help you to understand more about how important the family's job is.

Feelings and behaviour

 Send for the NSPCC film "Tomorrow's Parents", which provides an insight into how families can be helped to cope with the difficult feelings which may lead to treating children badly.

"I think a well behaved child should . . ." Complete this statement by collecting several sentences and then compare your list with several other people's lists.

Choosing how to behave

Look at your lists and then think carefully about the sort of behaviour you have described. Is it mainly for the adult's or for the child's benefit?

How do the people around you try to encourage you to behave in certain ways?

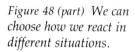

Figure 48 (part) We can choose how we react in different situations.

Figure 48 (continued)

We always have a choice about how we behave. Sometimes it is difficult to see what that choice is. It can also be difficult to make the choice. Occasionally situations we find ourselves in can be so serious that none of the choices is a pleasant one. It is, however, possible to get better, with thought and practise, at making choices and it is also possible to improve one's understanding of why other people choose to behave as they do.

Can you suggest why the people in figure 48 are behaving like this?

Which of these people's behaviour would you like to change if you could? Why? How could you alter their behaviour?

Who is most responsible for the situation in each case – the child or the adult?

Information on behaviour

There has been a study of how parents and children behave together in public:

"I carried out my own study in the streets, shops, and buses of a provincial city. I watched a series of adult–child pairs for three minutes each, all of them matched with another pair of people for comparison. I watched them on sunny afternoons, in places that were not crowded and not at peak hours, so that people were not busy hurrying, or dodging the traffic.

"The pairs that did not include a small child ranged from teenage to elderly. But whoever they were, within my three-minute observation period, four-fifths had some speech together, or at least a glance or a smile. All their behaviour towards each other was courteous".

Why do adults put such effort into getting on so well with each other and yet treat children in the following way:

"Seven adults crossed roads telling their children to look out or hurry, but none of them looked at the children they were speaking to. Five yanked the child by arm or hand. Four children tried to talk to adults who paid no attention. Three children had their clothes adjusted on buses without one word spoken."

The author suggests that "parents who are 'driven up the wall' by normal childish behaviour, which they make worse through ignorance of how to respond, think children are tougher than they are or ought to be toughened". She also suggests that it is difficult to enjoy children's company in a society that gives such little importance to the task of looking after children.

Have you seen this sort of behaviour? What do you think makes adults behave like this to children?

Understanding and helping

How we behave is often influenced by what we see around us and the way other people behave towards us. If we are encouraged and praised we tend to repeat an action. This is called "positive reinforcement". Society tries to discourage certain actions, such as vandalism, by "negative reinforcement", which can be anything from a telling off to imprisonment.

What sort of example were those adults setting those children?

Here are some situations where you might expect small children to behave badly:
1) a new baby in the family
2) walking past the sweets at a shop checkout
3) going to bed;
4) at home on a wet, rainy day.

Can you put yourself in a child's shoes and explain why you might misbehave in a situation like this? Can you also suggest some practical, realistic things an adult could do to improve the child's behaviour?

Are the children in figure 49 being naughty or not? What effect would each type of adult behaviour have on the child? Choose the adult's behaviour from this list: ignore, tell off, join in, smack (never hit a child while you are in a temper), laugh, pick up and move away, distract with another activity, shout, lose temper, or remove the child from company for a short while (such as putting him or her to sit just outside the room or on the lower steps of the house staircase for a few minutes with the light on and with the door open so that you can see him or her and he or she can still see you).

Remember – children need to be continually reassured that they are loved and cared for even though you might be displeased on this occasion.

Can you suggest other sorts of occasions when adults might use one

Figure 49 Children's needs and adults' needs can clash.

or more of these ways of behaving? Do you think some might be generally more successful than others?

One of the most important factors in young children's behaviour is their age. It is simply unreasonable to expect some things of young children. You cannot expect small children to share, keep a secret, sit still for long, or understand and remember the reasons why they should or should not do something. This would be asking the impossible!

Are you always proud of your own behaviour?

There are sometimes quite a lot of obstacles in the way of our changing our behaviour, even when we can see that it would be sensible to do so. Feelings of pride, habit, force of circumstances, other people's expectations of us, affect us all.

> That is not how we do it at home.

Can you think of a time when you have thought or said this? What might make someone continue doing something in the same way as their family, even though they know it might not be the best way?

Feelings of fear and jealousy can result in difficult behaviour. Have you never behaved in an unreasonable manner because you were so jealous?

What sort of things cause you to feel bad tempered and to behave badly?

Boys don't cry! Girls don't fight!

When adults were given the **same** baby to hold, firstly told it was a girl, and with the baby dressed in pink, and then told it was a boy, and with the baby dressed in blue, they held the baby differently and talked to it in a different manner. They were much more active with the "boy" and held "him" in a much more upright fashion. It seems

Figure 50 Real boys and girls behave like this.

that we do treat boys and girls differently whether we intend to or not.

If boys and girls behave differently could it be partly because of this different sort of treatment, begun in their earliest days?

Can you find any other examples of boys and girls being treated differently? Are their feelings always treated in the same way? Are they encouraged to behave in the same way?

Family rules

Every family will have different "no go" areas of behaviour. It is important not to have too many of these, and to insist on them firmly but without being unkind. All happy families need a few simple rules about behaviour to enable them to live happily together. Some of these rules may fit in with their culture or religion.

What sorts of rules do you and your friends' families have at home? Discipline is important in all sorts of situations. It can help small children feel happy and secure.

If you are entirely honest with yourself which do you really prefer – an undisciplined or a disciplined classroom?

When things go wrong

There are some sorts of behaviour which adults might not like, but which they really simply have to accept in children sometimes. These include things like waking up in the night, food fads, temper tantrums, getting bored easily, wanting to repeat the same thing over and over again, getting over-tired and over-excited, and comfort habits like sucking a thumb or hugging a blanket.

If parents feel that their children are so badly behaved that they have to use a lot of punishment, then it would be worth taking a fresh look at the whole situation, perhaps with someone else to help them. It could be that there are simply too many rules, or that the adult's expectations are too grown up; the child might be receiving insufficient attention and be behaving badly to get some; the adults might be setting him or her a poor example; or the child might be behaving badly out of boredom. There could be so many causes that an outside, experienced, sympathetic viewpoint might be a real help in putting things right. This could come from a health visitor, social worker, or perhaps a member of a "self-help" group of parents. Emotionally disturbed children are disabled in a very real way, so it is important that the situation is not just left.

If you have any feelings which worry or frighten you and you don't feel you can talk to anyone you know about them, then there is an organization called "Childline" which may help. You can telephone them on 0800 1111. You can talk to them about anything and you do not need to tell them who you are.

Remembering how we felt and behaved as children can make us more sympathetic and understanding towards the young.

Now try these

Describe what it means to behave in a social or antisocial manner. Give some examples of each sort of behaviour. How can a 4-year-old be helped to be social? Why is this important?

Can you describe what the children in the following situations really feel like? Can you remember those sorts of feelings?
Susan breaks a plate by accident.
Tony screams when Dad starts to put his toys away.
David wants the light left on at night in his bedroom.
Sally is misbehaving at a boring adult meal.
Catherine is begging Mum to throw her up again and catch her.
Richard looks longingly at the biscuit jar.

Suggest several acceptable, vigorous ways for children to work off their aggressive feelings. How do adults do this?

Try to explain how having a few rules helps us all to behave better towards each other, but how having a large number of rules can have the opposite effect.

106 Feelings and behaviour

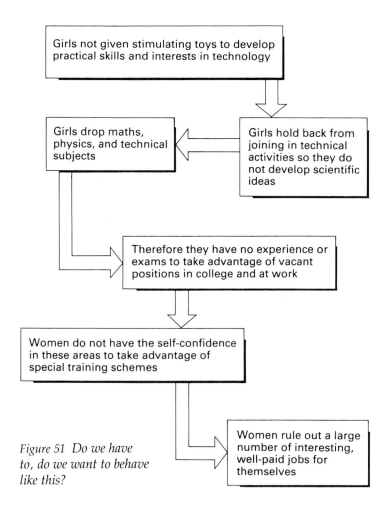

Figure 51 Do we have to, do we want to behave like this?

Look at the summary of an Equal Opportunities Commission advert in figure 51. How could girls' behaviour be influenced?
Look at figure 52. Do you think boys' behaviour could be influenced too?

PALS is short for Parents' Listening Service. It is a "self-help" group of parents who advertise a telephone number that angry and distressed parents can use. What sort of things might the parents of young children ring up about? How might another parent be able to help? Why do some parents prefer to speak to another parent on the telephone rather than talk to a social worker?

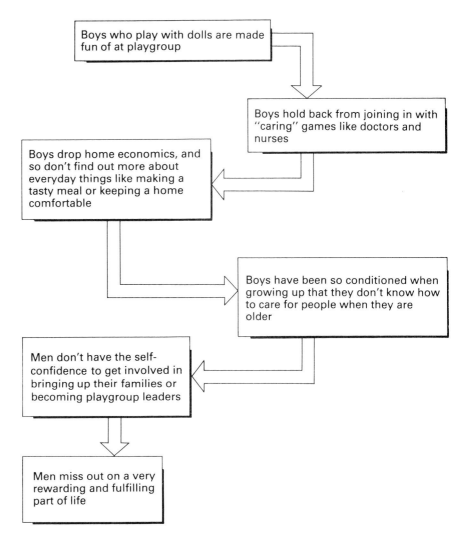

Figure 52 Do we have to, do we want to behave like this?

Carry out your own research by watching how adults behave towards children when you are "out and about".

Some adults get scared when children don't do what they tell them to do! Why do you think this is? How might the adults react because they are scared?

SEE ALSO

Health and illness for more about young children's behaviour. *Experts* for more about the sort of help that is available if families are really worried about any feelings or behaviour.

How Not to be a Perfect Mother (Fontana/Collins, 1986), by Libby Purves, is a book which describes a mother's feelings in a light-hearted way, and it would be worth while reading even a small part of it.

Invite some parents to come to school and discuss the sort of rules that families have. You might like to ask how they changed the rules at home as their children grew up. Which rules did they insist on most and why?

A nursery school teacher or a playgroup leader will be able to give you some good advice on how to handle children who behave in a difficult manner. Ask them to come and tell you about some real children and some real siuations.

Feet and shoes

Collect some thin card or thick paper and some talcum powder.

Send for information from some shoe manufacturers (such as those on pages 176 and 180).
Write to The Children's Foot Health Register (address on page 176).
Write to your district Health Education/Promotion Unit for information on the care of children's feet.

Shape and size

Find several people who wear the same size shoe as you. Draw round your feet and then draw round theirs. Cut out these feet and compare the shapes. Are they all exactly the same shape? How many differences can you spot?

It is because feet vary in shape as well as in size that children should have the width as well as the length of their feet measured (figure 53).

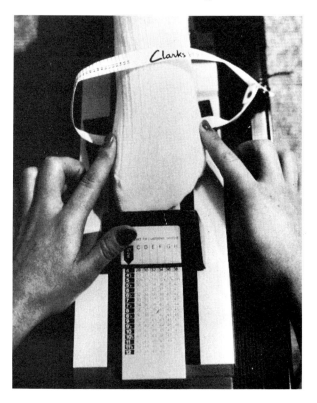

Figure 53 Do you remember having your feet measured?

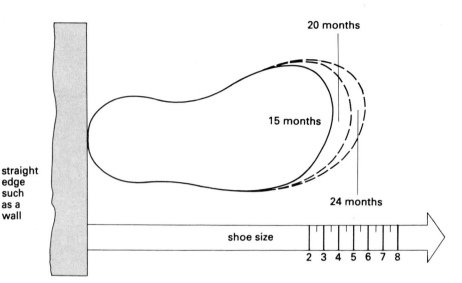

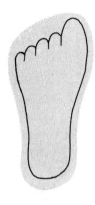

child

Figure 55

adult

Figure 56 Fashion can damage your health.

Figure 54 How often do children need new shoes?

Look at the rate of growth of the child's foot in figure 54. How often do you think her feet should be measured?

Look at some of the paper feet you cut out. Are they showing signs of having been mistreated?

Figures 55 and 56 show what happens to the foot in differently shaped shoes.

Look carefully at the shoes the people around you are wearing. Which parts of these shoes have been mis-shapen by the shape of the wearer's foot? These are the places to look at very carefully when you are buying shoes.

Have another look at all your paper "feet" and sort them into two piles. Put all those which have been undamaged by footwear into one heap, and then put all those which have had their shape changed by wearing shoes into another pile. Which are there most of? Which types of damage are most common?

Buying shoes

Children often grow out of shoes before they wear them out. This means that it can be expensive to provide them with shoes that always fit them.

Shoes can be bought from a shoe shop in your local high street, but can you think of any other places which sell shoes? Write a list and then put a star beside all those methods which enable you to have a child's foot measured.

How could you check to see if a shoe fitted a child yourself?

Sprinkle some talcum powder into your shoe and then carefully put your foot in, walk around, and then carefully take your foot out. Look inside your shoe. Is there a gap at the end around your toes? There should be at least one centimetre of talcum powder left in the end of a child's shoe to allow for growth. You can also use the measuring chart often printed in children's clothes catalogues.

Another way is to put the heel of the child's foot against a straight edge, like a wall, and then draw a line where the toe comes. Then put the child's shoe on top and draw a line to show where the end of the shoe comes to. Is there any room for growth left?

How accurate do you think these methods are? Do they allow for the width as well as the length of the foot?

These methods are particularly useful to know if you ever put a child in second-hand shoes. Because feet come in such a variety of shapes it is also important to check that second-hand shoes have not been worn so much that they have taken on the foot-shape of the last wearer.

Figure 57

New shoes, new shoes,
Red and pink and blue shoes,
Tell me what would *you* choose
If they'd let us buy?

Buckle shoes, bow shoes,
Pretty pointy-toe shoes,
Strappy, cappy low shoes;
Let's have some to try.

Bright shoes, white shoes,
Dandy dance-by-night shoes,
Perhaps-a-little-tight shoes;
Like some? So would I.

BUT

Flat shoes, fat shoes,
Stump-along-like-that shoes,
Wipe-them-on-the-mat shoes
O that's the sort they'll buy.

FFRIDA WOLFE

112   Feet and shoes

Trainers, wellington boots, and plastic shoes are also economical footwear.

What have you heard anyone say about wearing these for long periods of time? What are your feet like when you take off shoes and boots like this?

Figure 58 Going barefoot is an important part of some activities.

Up until about eighteen years of age it is possible to damage your feet without realising it, because it might not hurt. Up until this age the bones in your feet are still growing and hardening. Any damage you do cannot be undone. When babies are born they only have three real bones in their feet. The rest are made from cartilage and can be easily damaged by the slightest pressure. Even tight socks or a Babygro outfit which is too small can cause damage. Children do not complain about pressure or feel pain if their shoes are cramping their toes. The first signs of trouble are redness and corns.

Can you find a pair of shoes, perhaps in a catalogue, which you could recommend for a young child but which are not like the "stump-along-like-that" shoes described in figure 57?

Is it sometimes easier and more fun to do things barefoot (figure 58)? Care needs to be taken that there is nothing sharp on the floor if you are going to walk about barefoot.

Toddlers find it easier to learn to walk barefoot because they can balance and grip with their toes better. Children do not need to wear any shoes at all until they are taking several steps outside.

Now try these

State four things you should think about when choosing a pair of shoes for a child.

Suggest two ways of economising on the cost of providing shoes for a child. What should you be particularly careful about in each case?

Look at the "Children's Foot Health Register" that you sent for. What is special about the shops in this booklet? Are there any shops near you which are in this booklet?

Most of the people who need treatment for their feet are women. Why do you think it is women who are in such particular danger of having damaged feet? What could they do to avoid this damage?

Carry out a survey on today's fashionable shoe shapes. Do you think they are damaging feet at all?

It is such a waste of money. She never wears out her shoes.

What would you say to this Dad of a 3-year-old daughter?

114 *Feet and shoes*

Figure 59 Would some "flashy" shoes bought from a jumble sale and used for dressing up help this small girl?

Is there any way in which the situation in figure 59 could have been avoided? How should a responsible adult react to this child?

Find out the cost of several different sorts of children's footwear. There is at present no Value Added Tax on children's footwear because, as a government report said, "the price of children's footwear is an important factor in the context of foot abnormalities". What does this mean and do you agree?

What would you say to this manager of a shoe shop?

The X-ray pictures in figure 60 show the sort of permanent damage which can be done to feet by ill-fitting shoes. What are your feelings when you see distorted feet like these when people take off uncomfortable shoes: wear sandals or go barefoot?

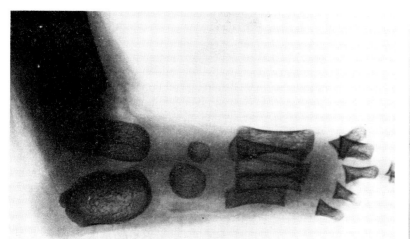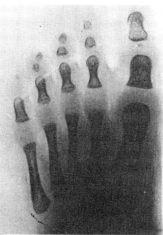

Figure 60 X-ray pictures of a permanently damaged foot (left), and a young child's undamaged foot.

Lots of young children like their slippers. Why do you think this is? Are they expensive? Do they cause any damage to the children's feet? Do slippers have any other advantages?

SEE ALSO

Clothes for more about what it is important to think about when you are dressing children.

If you or some of your group visit a playgroup or a playground you could do a survey of the types of shoes young children are wearing.

Your local shoe shop might be prepared to send someone to come and talk to you if you choose a time when the shop is unlikely to be busy. What sort of questions would you like to ask this visitor?

Food and drink

Write to your district Health Education/Promotion Unit (address on page 174) for information on the food pregnant women, babies, and small children should eat. You will also find it useful to ask them for information on the care of teeth.
Send for the leaflet "Food Additives" from the Ministry of Agriculture, Fisheries and Food (address on page 178)

My diet

Start by looking at your own diet. Write down everything you had to eat and drink yesterday, and then use *Food for Health* or a similar book to identify some of the nutrients which are in these foods. Why is each of these nutrients important to you?

More or less

It is important to remember that although each of these nutrients is important to us, that does not mean that the more we eat of each one the healthier we will be. Our need for each of these nutrients is different, and so we need to choose a diet which gives us each nutrient in the amount which we need it. At the moment, on average, our diets tend to be too high in fat, sugar, and salt and too low in fibre, and if we eat a large amount of processed food our diet will probably not contain enough vitamins and minerals.

A good diet is very important to the healthy development of a child's body and brain.

Sugar

Try to suggest several ways in which you might be able to eat less sugar. Which foods will you have to avoid? Might helping a child to avoid these foods be difficult?

If you run a fingernail against your teeth you will take off some of the sticky bacteria-containing substance called *plaque*. This is what we try take off when we brush our teeth. In our mouths starchy foods are broken down into simpler sugars which these bacteria eat. They then in time produce acid which attacks the enamel coating on our teeth.

Food and drink

BABY DRINK

Rosehip

INGREDIENTS:
Invert Syrup, Glucose Syrup, Rosehip Extract, Water, Vitamin C (0.42%), Citric Acid, Acidity Regulator (E331), Flavouring, Preservatives (E211, E223).

INSTANT BABY FOOD

Savoury Chicken Casserole
STAGE 2

INGREDIENTS:
Chicken, Carrots, Rice Flour, Cornflour, Onions, Soya Bean Flour, Celery, Potato Flakes, Peas, Dextrose (5.2%), Hazelnuts, Tricalcium Phosphate, Hydrolysed Vegetable Protein, Herbs.

Figure 61 These labels are from processed baby foods. Can you find similar ones?

It is therefore important that children do not go for a long time between eating a meal, a snack or a sweet and brushing their teeth.

Several baby foods claim to have "No added sugar". This only means the type of sugar we buy in bags in the shops called *sucrose*; but there are also other types of sugar called *dextrose, fructose, xylose,* and *maltose*. There are also products like honey, brown sugar, molasses, raw sugar, and natural sweeteners; but they are all sugar.

Look at the product labels in figure 61. What can you find out about the sugar in each product? The nearer the end of a list an ingredient comes the less there is of it in that food; but beware if there are several sugars near the end of a list of ingredients. What do you think the total sugar content might be?

Despite all this information some adults are still tempted to add sugar to baby food and to give young children sweets regularly. Why do you think this is? What could they do instead?

Salt

The salt we sprinkle on our food is called *sodium chloride*, and it can be one of the reasons why people get raised blood pressure. This is a significant factor in heart disease and is particularly dangerous for pregnant women. Salt can also be dangerous to babies as it may actually damage their kidneys.

Why do you think we add salt to our food? Why do manufacturers add it to so many of their processed foods?

Babies' tastebuds have not got used to the many and varied flavours of adult foods. They do not need or want the salty taste. Baby foods often taste bland to us, but this is not what they taste like to a baby. Adults who have cut down on their salt intake for a while find that they do not want to go back to using it and that foods they used to find acceptable now taste too "salty".

How could you start to retrain your tastebuds? There are some potassium-based salts on the market which are not bad for us, and since they taste less "salty"' they might help to retrain your tastebuds as well. These potassium-based salts do not cause raised blood pressure.

Fat

It is often difficult to cut down on fat intake because it can be quite difficult to spot the fat or oil in your foods. What sort of clues might tell you there was a fair amount of fat in a food?

People used to think that fat babies were healthy and appealing. What do you now think?

Use some food tables to help you make a list of the sorts of fatty foods of which small children should eat less. Which of these foods do you think it would be particularly difficult to avoid?

Fibre

Why do you think small children often get less dietary fibre than they need? There have been cases of children being rushed to hospital with such severe stomach pains that appendicitis was suspected. In fact the problem was acute constipation due to a diet very low in fibre.

What sorts of foods would young children like to eat that contain a fair amount of fibre (remember to try not to add salt, sugar, and fat)?

Early days

When in the womb a baby receives nourishment carried in the mother's blood. This travels along the cord to enter the baby's blood stream. It is therefore important that the mother is eating well so that she can supply her baby's needs. Because the embryo's needs are important from the very start of its life, but women do not know for certain that they are pregnant for the first few weeks, the woman should eat sensibly while she is trying to conceive. During pregnancy mothers are given, free of charge, iron and folic acid tablets. They also have to be sure to eat sufficient calcium and vitamin D. They should try not to put on too much extra weight and eat plenty of fibre and drink plenty of non-alcoholic drinks. Pregnant women and children under five are also provided with subsidised vitamin drops.

Iron and folic acid are essential for the formation of the haemoglobin in our blood. It is this which grabs the oxygen we breathe into our lungs and carries it to cells throughout the body. Because there is no iron in milk the baby builds up a six-month store of iron in its liver before it is born. Tablets, rather than an improved diet, are given to pregnant women because their need for iron and folic acid is so immediate, and because the absorption of iron from food is often low and slow. The absorption is helped by eating iron-rich foods with foods which are rich in vitamin C (ascorbic acid). Can you suggest three such combinations? Remember to keep the salt, sugar, and fat low and the fibre content high.

Vitamin D helps the calcium to form the baby's healthy bones and teeth. If the mother does not get enough of these for both her and the baby in the foods she eats her body will suffer because the baby will take what it needs from her store.

Which foods supply us with plenty of calcium? Do you eat these foods regularly? One way of getting enough vitamin D is to be outside in bright daylight or sunshine, and to let this light get to our skins.

Constipation and indigestion are fairly common minor ailments in pregnant women, and a diet high in fibre and with plenty of liquid will help with this. Also a diet rich in liquids puts less strain on the woman's kidneys. At each ante-natal appointment her urine will be tested to check that her kidneys are working satisfactorily.

Food and drink 119

Choices

In 1974 Britain was a bottle-feeding nation. Now at least eighty per cent of mothers start off by breast-feeding their babies because they are convinced that it is best for the baby. The immunity it provides and the fact that the contents of breast milk adapt to the baby's needs are important factors. No manufacturer of special baby milk powder would dispute that "breast is best", although baby milks are closer to breast milk than they used to be.

There are strict guidelines regarding the content and hygienic production of these milk formulas. If parents do decide to use bottles it is very important that they prepare and store the bottles hygienically. An upset stomach or gastro-enteritis is very serious in babies and is caused by bacteria. Bacteria find warm milk an ideal food!

Another disadvantage of using formula milks is the possibility of using too much powder and therefore giving the baby too many calories and also risking dehydration. It is essential to follow the instructions exactly.

When thinking about how to feed their new baby parents can get information and advice from books, leaflets, television, the health visitor and midwife, the doctor, and neighbours, friends, and family. Which of these might be the most powerful influences?

Figure 62 This sign is part of a scheme to help mothers when they are out with young children.

There is evidence to show that the majority of mothers breast-feed their babies whilst they are in hospital, but that some start to bottle feed when they get home. Why do you think this happens? What kind of support would help to prevent this?

The sign in figure 62 is displayed in places such as shops, toilets, and restaurants where there are clean, warm, adequate facilities for mothers to feed and change their babies. What would a father do if he were going out with his small child (figure 63)?

Figure 63

First meals

New babies are given a milk feed every three or four hours. How many "meals" is this per day?

Other foods should not and need not be introduced until the baby is about four months old. When this process of weaning starts only one food should be introduced at a time so that the parents know if a food disagrees with a child. To start with just a taste on the end of a teaspoon should be offered.

Gradually the quantity and the variety of the foods the baby is eating will be increased.

Baby rice, stewed and liquidised eating apple, boiled and sieved carrot, and potato are the sort of dishes many babies start off with.

Suggest two meals suitable for a one-year-old. By this age the child will be drinking from a feeder cup, and having nearly the same food as the rest of the family, and eating only three main meals a day.

Children should be encouraged to try and feed themselves, even though it will be very messy at first. They will be very proud of this new ability and will slowly begin to feel themselves an important part of the family.

How true do you think this is? Would it be true if a one-year-old child came to live with you and your family?

Slightly older children begin to want to exercise some control over what they will and will not eat. Did you have any food "fads" at this age?

It is impossible for a child to eat well in a family which eats a poor diet. Everyone might have to alter what they eat if the child is to eat well.

Figure 64 Empty tubs with clip-on lids, a feeder mug, a dish with suction base, shaped knife and fork, collapsible baby seat, and a plastic bib.

These fads can be very annoying for the adults because the child will only eat a few tried and trusted favourite foods. Most parents find if they do not make too much fuss about this and use clever ways to make sure the child is eating reasonably well that this stage passes.

How do you think the items in figure 64 could make mealtimes easier and more pleasant for both the adults and the children?

In what ways do you think it might be important for a family with young children to eat at least some of their meals together?

Comparisons

Try to conduct some of your own comparisons between bought and home-made baby foods. If you can get some real tasters all the better! Perhaps you know a family who would be willing to test out the foods for you, if you delivered them in little chilled pots ready for use?

Some foods which you could compare are bought and home-made fruit jellies, banana and apple purée, or liquidised cooked and mixed vegetables. The bought product could be dried or in a tin or jar. Be sure to produce your own labels for your home-made products to show the ingredients, cost, and how to use it.

The sort of things it might be useful to compare are the ingredients, the cost and quantity, the time taken, and the look and taste of the finished result.

How might freezers and microwaves help when organising children's meals?

Looking good

One of the very attractive things about lots of children's processed foods is their colourful, fun appearance and presentation. A great deal of this is achieved by using additives which we are now rather wary about. Can you provide healthy food which looks attractive (figure 65)?

Special concerns

There are several reasons why small children might have a special diet. Their parents might be vegetarians or have religious beliefs about food. The child might have an allergic condition, such as eczema or hyperactivity, which is improved if certain foods are avoided. Some babies are allergic to cow's milk. It is also advisable for all very young children to avoid foods which contain the cereal protein "gluten" so that coeliac disease is less likely in later life.

Some children might also have medical conditions which mean they have to have special diets.

122 *Food and drink*

Figure 65 A selection of home-made dishes suitable for small children, and with no added sugar or salt.

Children around the world

"Within a decade no child will go to bed hungry . . . no family will fear for its next day's bread and no human being's future and capacity will be stunted by malnutrition." This was said by Henry Kissinger in 1974.

The world is producing enough food to feed everyone, but in some countries most of the people are too poor to pay for it.

	Average daily calorie intake	Percentage of daily needs	Infant mortality rate per 1,000 live births	Life expectancy (years)
Ethiopia	1758	76	122	47
United Kingdom	3322	132	11	74

The concerns of people for food and drink in these two countries are very different. Can you describe what some of these differences might be?

> Congratulations to the lucky pupils of Newton Primary School where sweets, crisps, iced lollies, and sweet drinks have been banned by the Head Teacher.

Now try these

What should the tuck shop sell instead?

We do not like pregnant women to put on a lot of unnecessary extra weight.

How could a pregnant woman satisfy her hunger without putting on too much weight?
What other important facts should a pregnant woman know about her diet?

Why are women recommended to breast-feed their babies? What sort of things are likely to encourage a woman to keep on breast-feeding her child?

Look at the labels on foods like ice cream, squash, biscuits, instant dessert, and other types of foods which might appeal to children.
Now, using the information you sent for on food additives, say why they are in these foods.

Read this sentence from a research paper: "the fat cells made in childhood are with you all your life; the fewer you make then the fewer you will always have." How could we prevent children forming too many fat cells when they are small?

Imagine you have been asked to help with some simple cookery with some playgroup children. What could you cook with them that they would both enjoy making and eating but which would also be a healthy choice?

If you were going to improve your own diet in one way what would it be? How would you carry this improvement out? Why don't you give it a try!

Plan and pack a picnic tea for two 3-year-old children to eat in the garden. Make sure that it is enjoyable as well as being good for them, but do not spend too much time or money on it. Think carefully about the quantity of food you include and be adventurous with the presentation.

Suggest two interesting breakfast menus for a family with a 5-year-old and a $2\frac{1}{2}$-year-old child.

SEE ALSO

See the book *Food for Health* (in this series) for information about food for children and about additives.

Eat to Live, by Dodie Roe, published by Longman (1983), will give you information about the nutrients in food.

Your local district dietitian would make a very interesting speaker. Try to find out what a dietitian does and ask for some real stories about children who have been made ill by their diet.

Invite a breast-feeding counsellor from your local branch of the National Childbirth Trust (address on page 178) to come and tell you about this organisation's work.

Health and illness

Write to your district Health Education/Promotion Unit (address on page 174) for general information on positive good health such as diet, exercise, and not smoking; and also for information on topics such as cleanliness, care of teeth, head lice, worms, and childhood illnesses; and also for information on the post-natal care of a mother.
Write to the National Eczema Society (address on page 179) for details of this condition, and Astra Pharmaceuticals (address on page 175) for a booklet on asthma.
Write to "CLEAR" (address on page 176) for more information about how the lead around us can make us ill.

Growing up healthy

What does "being healthy" mean to you?

In small groups, draw a cartoon of a healthy and an unhealthy person. Label the things about them that show them to be unhealthy or healthy in your opinion. Discuss your cartoon with the rest of the group. Does your cartoon of an unhealthy person show someone who is miserable and is your healthy person happy? Some people think that health is as much to do with the mind as the body. Do you agree?

Look at the leaflets you sent for on asthma and eczema. People who have either of these can be healthy most of the time unless they have it very badly.

As we grow up we become more responsible for our own health. When we are babies we are washed and given clean clothes. As we get a little older we learn to wash ourselves with help, and then we are trusted to do it ourselves with occasional checks and reminders. Eventually we will become responsible for organising our own clean clothes and making decisions about when they are necessary, and still later we might be responsible for caring for other people's needs.

Look at the "Health life-line" in figure 66 (over the page), which shows the sort of things that concern people about their hair at different ages. Try to do your own "Health life-line" on another topic such as teeth or exercise.

One of the most important and simplest measures which has been taken to ensure the healthy development of children both in Great Britain, and more recently in developing parts of the world, is a system of development checks.

Parents are encouraged to take their babies to the clinic regularly to be weighed and to have their length and heads measured. This is also a

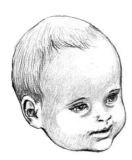
Wash hair carefully, because of "soft spot"; may get cradle cap.

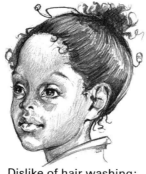
Dislike of hair washing; fine hair which tangles easily; own brush and comb; try not to make a fuss about hair cuts.

Stronger hair now; head lice may be a problem; may still need help washing hair.

Concerned about hairstyle and appearance; may be using colourants and perms.

Greying hair, and perhaps baldness.

Difficulty in washing own hair; hair may become very thin.

Figure 66

chance to discuss any difficulties such as feeding, crying, rashes etc.

There are also regular detailed developmental checks at the following ages, and these are some of the items on a local authority Child Health Service development chart. The health visitor or doctor is asked to tick the things that the child is able to do.

Six weeks: babies let their heads hang back when they are gently pulled up to a sitting position; they suck well; they smile; they are startled by sudden, loud noises and turn their heads towards the light. At this age the baby's hips are also checked and a blood test is carried out to ensure that the child can digest protein correctly.

Three months: baby holds rattle for a short time; watches own hands when lying down; gives squeals of pleasure; and when lying flat on stomach, lifts own head up.

Seven to eight months: baby can sit without support for a short period; tries to crawl; drinks from cup; reacts to mirror image; is apprehensive of strangers; has a two-syllable babble; and transfers toys from one hand to another. At this age the child's eyesight and hearing are also checked.

Ten to twelve months: the child can stand while holding onto furniture; can play clap-hands; can wave bye-bye; and can pick up small things between tip of index finger and thumb.

Eighteen months: they help an adult to dress them; throw a ball without falling; build a tower with three to four cubes; can say a few words; can walk upstairs with their hand held; and can understand simple orders.

Two years: child can kick a ball; can walk backwards; unscrews lids; builds a tower with six to seven cubes; can put on socks and shoes; asks for food, drink, and toilet; watches others play but does not join in; joins two or three words together into sentences; and is mostly dry by day.

Three years: child now able to walk on tiptoe, jumps off bottom step; builds tower of nine bricks; rides a tricycle; can dress fully except for buttons; joins in play; asks what, where, and who; and understands sharing.

Four years: child hops on one foot; likes imaginative play; tells stories; counts up to ten; asks why, when, and how; understands taking turns; and draws a person when asked to.

These checks are all based on the average performance of a very large number of children at a similar age. Although there would be no need to worry if a child did not do these things at exactly the right age, they could give a sign that something might be wrong early enough for action to be taken. As you can see these checks monitor a range of healthy development; physical, social, mental, and emotional.

These childhood checks are part of a much larger attempt to promote positive good health throughout the community. In later life such things as medical checks, well-woman clinics, and going to some trouble to look after one's own health all become important.

Six weeks after their baby is born all women have an important post-natal health check. You can find out from the Health Education/Promotion Unit leaflet the sorts of important things that are checked at this visit.

Looking after ourselves

There is a very worrying statistic that shows that there does seem to be a very strong link between poor health and poverty. Figures show that the number of children who die at birth is dropping, but that most of the success is amongst the wealthier families.

In what ways do you think poverty might stop us looking after our own health?

Our environment also plays a great part in our staying healthy. Sensible storage and regular collection and disposal of rubbish, clean water, control of pollution such as smoke, lead fumes, and noise, and the general cleanliness of our homes are all important.

There is evidence to prove that babies who are brought up in cigarette-smoking families absorb as much tobacco smoke as if they smoked themselves! These children also tend to suffer more from ear and chest infections.

There is another form of pollution which is unpleasant for all of us and particularly dangerous for children and which we could do a lot more about – this is the danger from dog faeces.

Toxocariasis is the disease caused by a threadworm which lives in the intestines of an estimated twelve per cent of dogs in Britain. The worm's eggs are excreted by the dog and if they enter the human body (this normally happens accidentally when children put their hands in their mouths) they may hatch and produce small insects which can travel to the eye and cause damage to the child's sight. This is treatable, but only if it is caught early enough. Dogs which are not wormed regularly and which are taken to walk in parks or fields, and on footpaths where children play are the cause. Children should always wash their hands after handling a pet, and always before eating, as some sort of protection against this sort of danger.

Can you suggest several things which are being done or which could be done about this sort of environmental health hazard?

Children in hospital

A quarter of all children under five have spent some time in hospital. Nursing a child is very different from nursing an adult, and many nurses in charge of children's wards have the Registered Sick Children's Nurse qualification. Hospitals are now expected to allow unrestricted visiting when children are in hospital, and to encourage parents to stay with their children as much as possible, including overnight. Parents can be a useful part of the nursing team. They can look after their child's everyday needs, provide company and amusement, maintain contact with home for the child, and explain what is going on and comfort the child. Children's wards also usually have a play leader and parents can help here too.

What sort of preparation could parents make so that if a child does have to go to hospital unexpectedly they will be well prepared and not too distressed? What sort of strain might having a child in hospital put on the rest of the family?

Now try these

Use the Health Education/Promotion Unit leaflets you sent for to find out more about first aid, symptoms of childhood illnesses, and suitable care. Now, in a small group, try to present the symptoms and treatment for one illness in cartoon form. *Mum – I feel funny* (Chatto & Windus, 1982) by Ann McPherson and Aidan Macfarlane is a whole book done like this.

Describe how health visitors try to encourage good health as part of their job.
In what ways do you try to look after your own health?

Write a list of points that describe a healthy, clean home environment for a young child.

> *Parents are important when children are patients in hospital.*

What is in the first aid boxes at your school? Are they easy to reach? What is important about the storage of medicines?

What sort of difficulties might parents have in trying to be there the whole time? How can a parent help their child best in these circumstances?

What sort of things make you feel better when you are unwell, perhaps in bed with a temperature? How might a 4-year-old be kept amused when ill in bed?

> *It is very important that all parents of young children know a lot about health matters.*

Find out more about head lice and human worms from the Health Education/Promotion Unit leaflets.
   Do you agree? What sort of matters should they know about and why?

How true is the statement "A happy home is a healthy home".?

There are children's books produced which set out to explain illness, dentists, doctors, and hospitals to children. Keep an eye open for these in bookshops and libraries. How do you think these might be used with children? Try to write a short illustrated story to prepare a 4-year-old for a visit to the opticians.

How might a pharmacist in a chemist's shop help you to stay healthy?

SEE ALSO

Diseases and immunisation for more information about this area of health and illness.

See the book *Home and Consumer* (in this series) for more information on environmental health and home safety.

You might be able to invite several parents with young children of different ages to visit you. You would then be able to see the gradual development as the children got older.

Perhaps a few of you might be able to visit the children's ward of a local hospital and assist the playleader. Report back to the rest of the group.

Invite a health visitor to come and speak to you about the positive good health side of their job. Ask to see the small toys, etc., they use when they carry out the development checks on children.

Home and going out

Write to your district Health Education/Promotion Unit (address on page 174) for leaflets showing how to make homes safer places and also for information on basic first aid.
Collect articles from magazines on how to improve the use or appearance of your home, particularly ones that refer to children's rooms. The Department of Transport (address on page 176) produces leaflets which give useful advice on travelling with children.

It's good to be home

What do you like best about your home and being at home? Homes are very important places to leave from and to return to. In small groups, take a large sheet of paper and stick a picture of a house in the centre. Now around the outside write down some of the things that would turn this house into home for you. Display your results so that the rest of your group can see them.

Poor housing conditions can lead to a great deal of misery and depression. They are thought to be one of the factors often involved in children's poor health. There are many families in Great Britain who are living in unsuitable housing (figure 67). Why do you think this is?

Children living in condemmed buildings

BED-AND-BREAKFAST BABIES

Tiny Tots near Main Road

Four-to-a-bed

Figure 67

What sort of things would make some housing unsuitable for a family with young children?

Home should be a safe, warm, comfortable, and pleasant place for children. If possible it should also be hard-wearing, easy to care for, and adaptable.

Suggest four things about a home which cannot be improved without a great deal of money. Then try and suggest eight things which can be improved quite cheaply. You might be able to renovate a piece of furniture yourself. Do not forget to take before and after photographs.

Being at home

There are some people who visit homes every day, such as the postman or woman and the milk and paper deliverers. Why do you think these people interest very young children so much?

Home is the place where young children spend most of their time. Describe four activities families with young children might enjoy doing together at home.

There are tasks which need doing in every home. How might it influence the children if they always saw their father doing the car cleaning and decorating or their mother always doing the washing and the tidying up?

Young children enjoy "helping" with these sorts of jobs. What might they be given to do alongside the adult who is car cleaning, decorating, washing, or tidying up? What sort of safety precautions would be necessary in each case? Try to write down two things the children would be learning as they helped with each of these jobs.

Pets

What pets did you and your friends have when you were little? What do you think young children enjoy about, and learn from having pets?

What sort of things should a family think about before getting a pet (figure 68)?

Gardens

Adults and children often enjoy gardens for different reasons. Write a list of five adult's garden activities and then five children's garden activities.

Copy the groundplan of a house and garden in figure 69 onto graph paper. In pairs, plan an ideal adult's garden and an ideal children's garden and draw them. When you compare these plans can you foresee any difficulties if both adults and children had to share each of your gardens? Are there any compromises possible which might help to solve some of these difficulties?

Home and going out   133

Figure 68 *Next time I think I'll get a gerbil.*

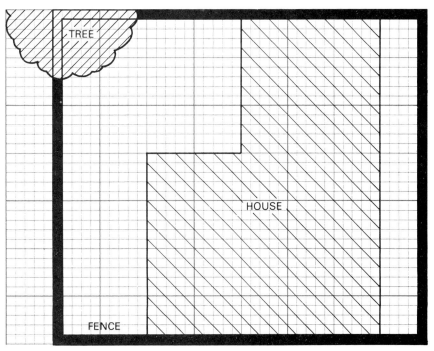

Figure 69

134 Home and going out

Figure 70 Would a child be safe here?

Figure 70 shows some of the dangers to avoid in a child's garden.

Children's rooms

It is not always possible for every child to have a room of their own, but where this is possible what do you think the advantages might be?

Pick out some of the good points about the rooms in colour pictures 4–7 (between pages 72 and 73). Are they safe? Are they easily adaptable as the children grow up? Is there plenty of easy-to-get-at storage space?

In a small group, write a list of all the sorts of things you need to store in a child's room. Beside each type of item suggest two ways of storing it, for example the child's toy cars could be put on display on open shelves or in an empty ice cream container in a cupboard.

How would you try to ensure that children could get at their toys, books, and clothes easily? Why is this important?

Risks and dangers?

Do you stick to safety rules all the time? Do you avoid dangerous situations? Do you try to improve dangerous situations you cannot avoid? Do you give safety lots of importance in your life? Try this questionnaire to find out more about what you feel about the everyday risks and dangers around you.

1. Do you always go out of your way to find somewhere safe to cross the road?
2. Do you ever go up the stairs without bothering to turn on the light if it is dark?
3. Do you always tidy up after yourself so that things are not left lying on the floor for other people to fall over?
4. If you were doing some cooking and you spilt something on the floor would you wipe it up straight away or would you leave it until it was convenient to do so?
5. Would you be prepared to pay more to buy dangerous products in bottles with child-proof lids?
6. Have you ever walked along a road alone, perhaps at night, when you know you should not have?
7. If someone tells you not to do something because it is dangerous does this put you off or does it make you more interested?
8. If a friend offered you a chance to have a little go at driving her car along a quiet road, even though you are under age and have no licence and insurance, would you be tempted?
9. Have you ever gone to any trouble to learn anything about safety or first aid?
10. "Compulsory rear seat belts would save lives". Would you be prepared to wear a seat belt whenever you sat in the back of a car?
11. You are babysitting one morning while Sam's parents visit his grandad in hospital. Sam is asleep in his cot but his mother has asked you to get an extra pint of milk from the milk deliverer. You hear the milkfloat going down the road and realise that you have just missed it. Do you quickly pop out of the house or not?
12. What ways do you use to stop yourself losing control when you are in a very frustrated and angry mood?
13. Can you think of any times when you have asked for help with something important? Do you find it easy or difficult to ask for and to accept help?

Discuss your attitudes to these sorts of situations in a group and then ask the group to tell you how they would describe your attitude to risks and dangers. They could use words like "cautious", "foolhardy", "sensible", "responsible", or "uncaring".

In every situation we all have a choice as to how safely we act. Here are three requests from a 3-year-old child: "I want to go and play on the pavement with the other children", "I want to go on that big climbing frame", and "I want to help you cook the dinner". How do you think an adult should react to these and similar situations?

Do some of your group differ in what they consider to be too dangerous for children?

Learning to cope

On an average day we reach, climb, carry, go up and down, use fuels and equipment and dangerous products from bleach to hot cooking fat.

There is no magic age when children can suddenly cope sensibly. A great deal will depend on the situation they live in. A child who lives in a bungalow will probably learn to cope with stairs later than other children; and a child is probably ready to learn to use scissors if they want to cut something out, can use their hands carefully, understand the words "sharp" and "careful", and can concentrate for a short period of time.

What might you look for in a child if you were trying to decide whether it was safe to let them sit on a high stool, sleep in a bed without a guard, go and wash their hands by themselves, use a fairly sharp knife, or climb a tree?

What sort of things should young children be taught to try and help to ensure their safety amongst other adults and children?

Up to about seven or eight years of age (but this is a decision each parent has to make) children should not be allowed out without an adult at all. After this they should be seen across busy roads and always be with several other children.

However, children should be gradually allowed more freedom. Having a say in decision-making and being used to being well organised are two skills which will help them when they are making decisions about their own safety. How could parents encourage these skills in children?

Children who say that certain individuals make them feel uncomfortable should always be listened to carefully and sensitively. They should be taught that they have the right to feel comfortable when they are with other people and that **NO-ONE**, not even those in authority over them or their relations, has the right to approach them or touch them in any ways they do not like. They should be encouraged to come and say if anything like this ever happens to them.

Adults often tell children "Don't go with strangers" or "Don't take sweets from strangers". This is good advice, but how would you explain who was and who was not a stranger to a young child?

Pictures 11 to 16
Grandparents are all sorts of different people. What do you think these people feel about being grandparents?

Pictures 17 and 18
Toys like dolls, jigsaw puzzles, and Noah's Arks have been popular with young children for many years. When you look at these antique ones and the modern versions can you think of any reasons why they are such successful toys?

Pictures 19 to 22
These children are all completely involved with what they are doing. They are "in a world of their own". Please do not disturb them! Can you describe what each child might be feeling and thinking?

Going out

What sort of precautions do you think should be taken in the following situations?
taking a 3-year-old to playgroup along a busy road
collecting a 5-year-old from school by car
allowing a 10-year-old to go out to the playground
allowing a 12-year-old to go out for the morning shopping
allowing a 15-year-old to go to a disco
adults returning home late at night on public transport.

The Tufty club visits mother and toddler clubs, playgroups, nurseries, and infant schools but they do not teach the Green Cross Code to the very young children. Instead they recommend that these children should always have an adult with them when they go out. Why do you think road safety officers give this advice?

Eating out

It is often said that families on the Continent take their children out much more than people in Great Britain do, especially for meals. Why do you think this is so?

Where have you seen young children eating out with their families? What difficulties have you noticed?

Children enjoy going out to eat. Might there be any opportunities for them to learn anything new whilst they are eating out?

There is quite a lot being done to make it easier to take children out to eat in this country. Have you seen any of the things shown in figure 71 (below and over the page)?

Figure 71 (part) Enjoying a meal out together.

Figure 71 (continued)

Travelling with children

What are your memories of journeys when you were a child? Why might some families have to go on long journeys occasionally?

Here are some arrangements families might make if they were travelling with children:
travel by car at night
break the journey quite often
let the airline know they are travelling with small children
travel by train.
What might be the advantages and disadvantages of these arrangements?

It is very important to ensure that children are as safe as they can be when they are travelling in cars. By using the information you collected at the beginning of this Topic and by visiting shops which sell a variety of car seats, write a report which would be helpful to a family with young children. Do not forget to include some information about **always** using the car seat or seat belt properly. What might prevent adults from doing this? Many of these pieces of equipment have the British Standard Kitemark on them. What does this mean?

Young children might also travel in friends' or relations' cars and coaches. How might their safety be ensured in these vehicles?

Now try these

Some families have to move house every two or three years. What sort of things do you think it would be important to try to do to make the house feel like home as soon as possible?

> Damp, cold, overcrowded housing conditions make it impossible to provide young children with a healthy happy home life. They can therefore cost this country a great deal of money.

What sort of "costs" do you think these might be?

Gran is drinking a cup of coffee while she is holding her baby grandson; Mum is in a rush to get the children bathed and forgets to check the temperature of the water; Dad leaves 2-year-old Graham playing at the sink while he answers the door; and 16-year-old John leaves a hot electric kettle on a low table in the room next to his young sister's. Without intending to, what sort of risk are these people exposing young children to? Suggest ways to make the situation safer in each case.

> You can be too careful with children. If you mollycoddle them they will grow up less able to cope with real life.

> You can never be too careful with children. It is important to try to make sure they are safe every minute of the day.

What do you think?

> When I had my accident I heard them say... "I've told him and told him not to touch that tool box." "I kept meaning to get around to dealing with that trailing flex." "I didn't even know he could reach that shelf."

Why do you think these adults did not make the situation safe in time?

What sort of responsibilities could a 4- or 5-year-old be expected to carry out with a pet? What sort of encouragement and help might they need? Discuss whether you think goldfish, gerbils and rabbits make suitable pets for small children.

Why should:
a sandpit be covered when not in use
children be discouraged from picking and eating things in the garden
the garden be easily visible from the house if young children are playing in it
paddling pools be emptied when they are not in use
garden gates be locked shut
garden chemicals be locked away?

> He does the cooking, washing, and ironing and she does the decorating, gardening, and the car. Their children must be really confused!

What do you think?

Carry out your own safety investigation at a playgroup or nursery. What sort of accidents are small children most likely to have?

Try to visit some gardens which belong to families with young children. What sort of practical difficulties do the families have with making sure their children are safe when they are playing in the garden?

SEE ALSO

See the book *Home and Consumer* (in this series) for more information about accidents in the home.

Invite your local road safety officer to come and tell you about the work they do with the under 5-year-olds.

Some local authorities have home safety officers too, who could give you a great deal of information and some real life stories. Or you could organise a competition amongst yourselves to see who can design the best poster to encourage adults to be more aware of one aspect of safety with young children. Decide first what you are going to be looking for when you judge the competition.

You might be able to invite a police officer to come and tell you about the sort of things they tell young children to try to make them more safety conscious.

Playing

Send for information on children's play from the Pre-school Playgroups Association (address on page 179).

When was the last time you learned while you played? This is a satisfying and rewarding thing to do as, for example, when you learn a new skill such as how to crochet, dribble a ball, or windsurf. We also learn while we play games. We learn the rules, how to play with others, and how to handle both winning and losing. Play is not something that only children can do. Do you know any people who are adults who do a lot of playing? How do you think they benefit from this?

Remembering what it feels like to play

Do you know any games children play? Can you play hopscotch, skipping, jacks, skittles, or pick up sticks? When was the last time you did any of these?

This sort of playing needs only basic equipment but you do need friends, space, and time in which to do it.

Look at colour pictures 19–22 (between pages 136 and 137) to see some more children playing. Children spend most of their day playing.

What is play for a child? Is it: important, trying hard, having fun, wasting time, boring, competitive, mucking around, organised, essential, helpful to understanding, expensive, noisy, tiring, and private? Put these in columns headed 'Play is' and 'Play is not' and add some more words of your own to this list.

Play is part of each child's normal, healthy development and it is essential to the development described in the chart on page 126.

Where can I play?

Children do most of their playing at home, but from a very early age they like the toys and company of a parent and toddler club. These are usually run by the parents on a fairly informal basis, and are often good for both the adults and the children.

Try to visit a parent and toddler club. What do you think both the children and the adults gain from these? Why might it be difficult for a lone father to fit in?

Slightly older children often go to a playgroup. These started as a few children meeting in someone's home, and were intended to be just a stop-gap measure until pre-school or nursery education was provided for every child by the government. However, up to now this situation has not come about. Both nursery classes and playgroups provide young children with plenty of space, people, opportunities, and facilities.

Look at the following comparison of nursery classes and playgroups. How many differences can you spot? Try to explain the importance of two of these differences.

Local Authority nursery class	*Playgroup*
Run by the Local Education Authority.	Run by a committee of parents who may join the Pre-school Playgroups Association for advice, practical help, and insurance.
The adults present are nursery school teachers, nursery nurses, helpers, and sometimes parents.	These are usually run by a trained leader who might be a nursery nurse or someone who has been on a Pre-school Playgroup Association course. There are also helpers, and parents help on a rota basis.
These are often housed in purpose-built premises, and can be attached to a school.	These can be found in a variety of premises such as village halls, youth clubs, and community centres.
Parents do not have to pay to send their children, but the availability of places is usually very limited. There are also some privately run nursery schools.	The parents pay to run these with a charge for each session and with fund-raising events. Some receive small grants from the social services and from the Local Education Authority. A few subsidised places are usually available. Playgroups can usually be quite flexible about putting on extra sessions to meet the demand.
For 4–5 year olds.	For 3–5 year olds.
Normally there are five half-day sessions for each child.	There are normally a couple of half-day sessions per week for the younger ones and a few more for the older children.

Legally children do not have to start school until the beginning of the term following their fifth birthday, but some start at four years + one day. There is some flexibility to allow for the "readiness" of the child.

I like doing this

If we group some of the different sorts of play children enjoy we will be able to see clearly what it is they enjoy about them and also what they might be learning.

1) **New sounds** can be great fun. The important thing is to encourage children to listen carefully. Music shops sell well-made xylophones, bells, whistles, tambourines, and wooden maracas. It is also possible to make sound toys yourself by, for example, sawing a coconut in half. Or you could use a glass to tap on gently, or you could put beans, etc. in see-through margarine tubs or lemonade bottles. (These have the extra advantage of letting the children see what it is that is making the sound.) Music making can be shared by everyone and it can be used to help children express how they feel. It can also be used as a background to movement games.

Figure 72 Water is fun to play with.

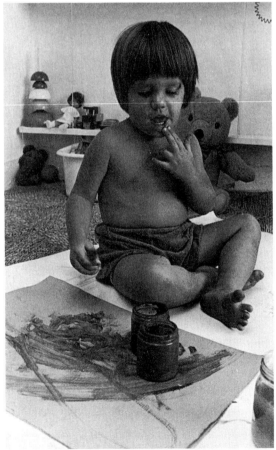

Figure 73 Not to be disturbed!

Why do you think it is important to encourage young children to listen carefully?

In your group try to make a variety of sound toys then record a story with added sound accompaniment. Your toys must be safe and strong and make pleasing, interesting noises.

Can you think of any songs which are not traditional nursery rhymes but which you and young children would enjoy singing together? You could use your sound toys to accompany you. Maybe you know some songs with actions which children would enjoy.

2) **Water** can be played with in a great many different ways. It can be warm, cold, moving, still, bubbly, and coloured.

How many different ways are there to play with the objects in figure 72? What sort of things would small children be discovering while they played?

3) **Paint, clay, dough, chalks**, and **crayons** all help children to express feelings and ideas and to create things that are truly theirs. They can also experience new textures and colours (figure 73).

Try to hold your own play session where you can enjoy doing some of these things. Make some of your paint very watery and some very thick. You can make paint thick by mixing it with flour or wallpaper paste.

4) Coordination is encouraged by the sorts of toys in figure 74 which help children to learn to use their eyes and their hands together, and to use both hands at the same time.

Figure 74 Threading and posting toys.

Figure 75 A movement class for young children.

5) The larger activities in a movement class, such as the one shown in figure 75, help children to learn to control their bigger movements, and to develop their strength and balance. It also develops the children's ability to concentrate, and their self-confidence.

Why might it be difficult to provide some of these sorts of play at home?

Some other types of play include games with rules which can be played alone or together and imaginative play with doll's houses, farms, and domestic toys, etc., which help children understand feelings and ideas through imitation and make-believe. Posting boxes, jigsaws, and matching games help them to tell the difference between shapes, size, and colours.

Play is important

It is through play that children explore the world around them. They do this in many different ways. You will be able to see them doing this if you watch a group of them playing at dressing up. Watch them "step into the role" of a doctor, a father, a teacher, etc. Listen to what they say and how they say it. Watch their face and body movements. They are not "acting". They are unconcerned about any audience who might be watching them. They are exploring what it feels like to be these people. They can also explore what it feels like to be angry, sad, ill, and so on, in a similar way.

They also explore how things work and what happens if they do something. For example, a 3-year-old might think that a stone would float because it looked like a boat. Not until they have actually put the stone in the water and seen it sink and carried out many similar "experiments" do they begin to understand fully about floating and sinking. This sort of play is clearly the very beginnings of understanding science.

Children gain a lot of understanding about the world through their play so we should look very carefully at the things we give them to play with. When you visit a nursery class or a playgroup or a small child at home, try asking yourself which toys reflect the fact that our society is made up of a number of different cultures. Are any of the dolls black? Do the books show girls as mechanics or boys as nurses?

It is very easy to break a child's concentration or to deflect them from the sort of play they wish to do. Adults should be very careful about disturbing children at play, joining in, or telling them how to play. This does not mean that you should never do these things but rather that you should think twice before doing so and that you should not do them regularly.

Enjoying playgrounds

In a society which seems to be very aware of the everyday dangers there are to children such as medicines, seat belts, and fire guards why do we tend to ignore the dangers present in playgrounds?

Playground hazards include hard swing seats which can cause serious head injuries; slides which are often the height of first floor windows with hard concrete or tarmacadam underneath them; and moving pieces of equipment such as rocking horses and roundabouts which cause the sort of accidents where children's limbs get crushed.

Most of the accidents in figure 76 could be avoided. Good design of the site and safe equipment, properly installed and well maintained,

Figure 76

Playground closed after boy is hurt

Danger playgrounds: council to act soon

'Killer' climbing frame ban urged by parents

SWINGING TO DEATH IN THE PLAYGROUND

Playground accidents that need not happen

Peril of playground death traps

are important. There is no shortage of ideas for improved playground design and equipment.

Go and look at a playground near you and check it for safety using this checklist. The list is adapted from one used by a national campaign which tried to improve all our playgrounds.

Playground Safety Checklist

Name of playground ....

Who owns and runs this playground? ....

SURFACE
What sort of surfaces are there? (* would mean that there is a small amount of this surface, **** would mean that there is a great deal of this type)

concrete	tarmac
paving	grass
sand	rubber

Describe any other surfaces which are present ....

....

SUPERVISION
Is this playground supervised? YES/NO
Is the supervisor trained in:
First Aid YES/NO
Work with children YES/NO
Has any provision been made for adults while they supervise their children (such as seats)? ....

DANGEROUS EQUIPMENT

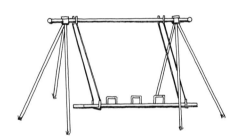

Figure 77 Dangerous pieces of playground apparatus.

Are there any of the pieces of equipment in figure 77, which have been proved to be dangerous, in this playground?

SAFE EQUIPMENT CHECKS
Are all upright supports firm? YES/NO

Where can you see rust? ....

Where can you see damaged timber? ....

Can you see any frayed or worn ropes? ....

Can you see any sharp edges? ....

What sort of material(s) are the swing seats made of?

metal   rubber

wood   rigid plastic

At what height are the swing seats? ....

How long is the run-out at the end of the slide? ....

Does the slide face the full heat of the sun? YES/NO

How deep are the sides of the slide? ....

OTHER HAZARDS
Please give details of things such as if the playground is beside a main road with inadequate fencing and gates, if it is in a secluded area of a park, or if there has not been enough thought given to keeping dogs out of this children's area. ....

....

....

Now try these

In pairs try to describe a situation where you might join children in their play and say what you might have to offer to their playing. Now describe two situations where you would try to leave the playing children alone.

Check a number of local playgrounds, using the Playground Safety Checklist (page 148), and prepare a report. Who might be interested in seeing this report?

Using the information you received from the Pre-school Playgroup Association choose one form of play and carry out an investigation into it. Why do children enjoy it? What do they need for this sort of play? What are they learning while they are playing? How can an adult help?

Write an account of a child, or a group of children, you have watched playing.

Describe three sorts of accidents that could happen in a playground and say how they could have been prevented.

Design your own playground and label the safety features you have included.

What sorts of play do children do at a playground? Make a list.

There are not enough local authority nursery class places for every small child. Should there be? Do you think all adults would be willing to pay more in their taxes and rates for this?

Some parents do not send their children to a playgroup or nursery class. Why do you think this is? Should they be encouraged to do so?

How would you organise some waterplay for two or three small children at home during a cold winter's day?

Choose one type of play and explain why this sort of play is important for children and state what would be needed in order to provide it.

Carry out a survey amongst the younger pupils in your school or in some top junior school classes. How many children have had playground accidents? What sort of accidents were they?

SEE ALSO

Health and illness for a chart on healthy development.
Toys to find out more about what children like to play with.

See the book *Home and Consumer* (in this series) for more information about home safety.

Visit a nursery school or playgroup to help you to learn about children playing. Each time you go try to look especially at one thing. On one visit you could concentrate on how the building has been designed or organised to make it safe, pleasant and convenient for small children. Look out for small furniture, high door handles, locked gates, low shelves and hooks and get down to the children's level so that you can see what things look like from there! The next time you visit you could concentrate on looking at one type of play. Ask yourself questions like what sort of preparation the adult has had to do first, how long do the children spend on any one activity, and how is the clearing up organised? On another occasion you could study the relationships between the children and the adults or the children themselves. Another important area to look at is the organisation that goes on behind the scenes. How is arriving and going home time organised? When do the children have a drink? Who decides what the children will do?

Talking

Collect a variety of different sorts of nursery rhyme books. Collect pictures of lively scenes from magazines, which have plenty to talk about in them.
Send for leaflets from your district Health Education/Promotion Unit explaining how and when children start to talk, such as the leaflets which go with the film "Hello Baby".

Talk, talk, talk

What do you use the spoken word for most? Write a list of several different important reasons for speaking such as asking, explaining, discussing, telling, and expressing feelings, and so on. Now try to note which ones you use most during a period of a few hours. Could you have managed without talking? What might have been the disadvantages?

Have you ever played the game where you have to get an idea or object over to someone else without talking? Is this easy to do?

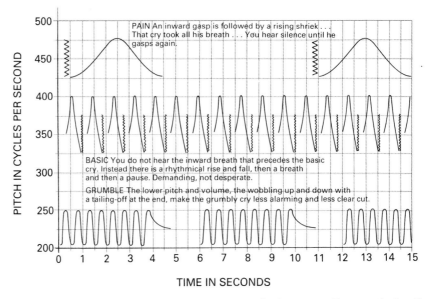

Figure 78 Typical cries. The baby's repertoire of cries grows. Presented visually from a sound spectrograph you can see the differences in volume, pitch, and rhythm in three typical ones.

Listen carefully

As the spectrograph readings in figure 78 show, even babies can communicate their needs. So probably the main reason for them learning to talk are that it is such a pleasurable thing to be able to do. They do not want to be left out. It is therefore important that anything that we do to help them learn to talk should not take the pleasure out of it. Happy children talk willingly. If children are upset they are quite likely to refuse to talk. What are your most important reasons for talking? Is it just to get what you want or is it to be in the middle of what is going on, understanding and contributing to it?

From the very start of their lives babies show that they are listening to the sound of human voices by their reactions. They do not turn to look where the voice is coming from until they are about two months

Figure 79

old but before this they do react, particularly to the sound of their parents' voices. They might stop crying or just lie still and listen. By about the age of three months it is possible to have a "conversation" with a baby because they will be quiet, listen to you, and then gurgle a response and wait for your answer. Between three and six months babies start to use their voices a lot more to accompany their actions but it is not until they are about one year old that they start to use any real words. Babies begin to grasp the meaning and point of language long before they can speak and use it. They do this by watching how we use it. This means that how we talk to even very young babies is very important.

By their second birthday children are normally saying about 200 words. They will now start to put two or three words together, but they do not always do this correctly. The best way to help them now is to repeat it back to them sometimes to show that you have understood and to let them hear it said correctly (figure 79).

There is no point in correcting a 2-year-old child's grammar because the rules are too complicated for them to understand. You have learned all this, but if you try to say what the past tense of each of these verbs is: it sinks, it happens, it sits, it comes, it looks, and it runs you will see how complicated our language is. Now do you see why small children often say "it sinked, it runned, and it comed"?

Learning your first language(s) (some children are lucky enough to be brought up bilingual) is not like learning a foreign language at school. You do not need "lessons". Children will sort out all the difficulties for themselves eventually if they hear the language spoken correctly and clearly around them and to them. This is such a good way of learning language that teachers of foreign languages sometimes try to mimic it by "immersing" their students in a language.

Pre-school children begin to use language for difficult tasks such as remembering what has happened in the past, predicting what might happen in the future, and to express thoughts, ideas, and feelings. They begin to talk about things which are not actually present. These are important things to encourage because if we could not talk about what has happened in the past we could not learn from it. Being able to imagine what might happen in the future also saves us from doing things we might otherwise regret, and it lets us anticipate what the consequences of our actions might be. People who cannot find the words to express their thoughts, ideas, and feelings find life difficult to cope with and are frustrated. The development of children's language goes along with the development of their thinking.

Young children need toys and situations which will stimulate their imagination and they need to talk about what they are, have been, and will be doing and seeing. This conversation will in turn give them more new ideas and words. Doesn't it sometimes help you to understand a new idea if you speak it out loud? To be able to think, to use our intelligence, we need to be able to use language in a controlled way.

Figure 80 Bought and home-made books with many parts.

This is why speech therapy is very important to young children who have difficulty in talking clearly. Do you know anyone who has been to see a speech therapist? What sort of help were they given?

Fun with language

What should a good nursery rhyme be like? Get together with one or two others and try to describe a good nursery rhyme.

How many nursery rhymes can you recite? Does it matter how you say them when you are with children? What sort of chances are there in a normal day to say nursery rhymes with children? What do you think children like about nursery rhymes? What do you like about hearing a favourite old song again and finding that you can remember the words?

What types of nursery rhyme books are available? Can you group them? Are they all for the children to use? How could you use a nursery rhyme book with young children?

Choose a nursery rhyme and try to illustrate it with a lively picture which could have a moving part for the child to work, as in figure 80.

Practise speaking the nursery rhyme out loud. Perhaps you could add some simple sound effects and then record it. Listen to the result carefully. Is it clear, lively, and fun? Would it tempt a child to listen carefully and to join in?

Now try these

Practise doing the following as if you were talking to a small child. Talk clearly and do not forget to make it memorable and fun by overacting!

a) Describe an elephant.
b) Offer a choice between cornflakes or toast for breakfast.
c) Explain why you need some help in putting the toys away.
d) Express delight at seeing the sun.
e) Predict what you might do after tea.
f) Instruct on how to wash your hands.

Talking involves using the facial muscles to make different shapes and thus produce different sounds. Young children enjoy it when adults make unusual sounds with their mouths. Can you click your tongue, blow a raspberry, make a "pop" with a finger in your mouth, whistle, and so on?

Try to make up a commentary using lots of interesting words that a parent might say to a child as they watched a herd of cows walk along the road going to be milked.

Talking to young children is a waste of time because they can't understand you and anyway I feel silly doing it.

What might you say to this person?

Using your pictures out of magazines with plenty to talk about in them, attach a thick paper tab to the bottom of each. Cut a "thumb-hole" out of the open end of a large second-hand envelope. Put the picture into the envelope with the tab sticking out. Now slowly pull the picture out.

What could you discuss with a small child as you did this?

Why do you think some adults occasionally find it difficult or boring to talk to children? How can the adult make this easier, more interesting, and more pleasurable for themselves and the children?

A "pun" is "the humorous use of a word with different meanings". Do you know some simple jokes using puns which you think young children might enjoy? (For example: "When is a door not a door?" "When it's ajar.")

You might be able to collect some tape recordings of young children of different ages talking, if you ask their parents to help you. Recordings like this are as good as photographs at bringing back memories. When you listen to the children you could try and think of ways of helping the child to continue the conversation.

Try to practise some of your new skills on a young child, but remember it must always be fun. Take some "discussion starters" with you, such as your illustrated nursery rhyme or your pictures in envelopes.

Listen to yourself a little when you are discussing things with your friends. Is there anything you have learned which you can start to use straight away, such as the ability to listen carefully or to help someone express their feelings? Choose an unnamed person who you think uses language particularly well and describe how they do this.

Try to make up your own nursery rhyme. Get started by writing down a selection of interesting sounding words such as "drip, drop, plip, plop, slip, slop". Or you could try to put new words to a familiar nursery rhyme tune.

SEE ALSO

Books and television, as a great deal of conversation can take place quite naturally as you share a book with a young child or watch a television programme together.

Go to a local library and ask if they have a section of books for adults about children. Can you find a book or a chapter in a book about children's speech and their talk? Skim through and find a part which really interests you, or links up with something else you have learned. Perhaps you could find out more about a speech therapist's work?

Invite someone who has a great deal to do with children, such as a nursery school teacher or playgroup leader, to come and tell you about how they encourage young children to express themselves in words.

Toys

Collect lots of information about different sorts of children's toys from magazines, catalogues, and toy advertisements on television.
Collect some paints, paper, glue and a selection of cardboard boxes.
The Toy Libraries Association (address on page 179) will also send you information.
Send for a free video, called "Two too many", from the Advertising Standards Authority (address on page 175). It shows how a young lad feels about a particular toy he sees advertised.

Make it yourself

Children can turn lots of things into toys. The bubbles on a bowl of water, a set of keys, an elastic band, the tube from the centre of a kitchen paper roll, and empty cardboard boxes all make good toys.

Sometimes children have only to sit inside a box you have just emptied the shopping out of for them to become an engine driver or a racing car driver. At other times they might need more to spark off their imagination or to continue their game. Sometimes adults have the time and materials to make something special for them and they enjoy this. At other times they would rather adults did not interfere, perhaps they want to add their own make believe steering wheel and gear lever.

Imagine you are in this situation. The 2-year-old twins are having their morning sleep. You have tidied up, had a drink and a sit down and started the mid-day meal. What new toy(s) can you quickly make which will please them and also encourage them to use their imagination? Use the cardboard boxes, paper, paints, and glue you collected. You may also use any other things which you think would be readily available in this situation. Do not try to do anything too difficult because they will be waking up soon! How do you think they will play with your toy? If possible let a young child play with your toy. Did they enjoy themselves? How could you improve your toy? Should you contribute to their playing? If so, how could you do so?

There are also rather more permanent, elaborate toys which can be made out of cardboard boxes. These take considerably more time and effort to do but would last longer and do not cost a lot (figure 81, over the page).

Figure 81 A house made from a box.

Good toys

Carry out a survey amongst a group of 11 to 12-year-olds to find out what were their favourite toys when they were younger. Can you see any pattern in your results?

There are so many toys to choose from that it can be difficult to select the right one.

Your local library will have several catalogue-type books which will suggest well-designed and safe toys. Sometimes these books suggest toys suitable for children of a certain age, or they divide the toys up into groups to indicate the sort of activity they involve. You could also ask to see a copy of the magazine *What Toy*? What criteria do toys have to meet to be "highly recommended" by this magazine? Toy companies also produce lots of free information to encourage people to buy more toys.

Children learn to do the same things at roughly the same age. It is therefore often possible to recommend toys as being suitable for children of a certain age (figure 82).

Look at the catalogues you have (and any real toy boxes you might be able to have a look at in the shops) and using the chart on page 126, which shows you the normal development of most children, choose a child of a certain age and produce a poster showing which toys are recommended for them and say why you think this is so.

There are also toys which generations of children have enjoyed playing with (see colour pictures 17 and 18, between pages 136 and 137).

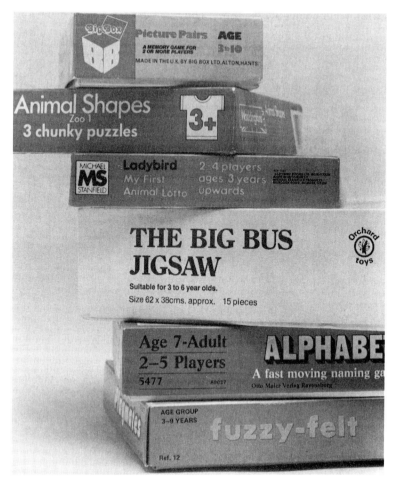

Figure 82 These toys are recommended for a certain age range.

Buying toys

There are a great many things to think about when buying toys. Here is a ten-point checklist of questions to ask yourself:

1 Is the toy safe?
It is illegal to sell a toy which is not safe. The law covers such things as: the amount of harmful metal in the paint, sharp points and edges, the attachment of things such as eyes, electrical safety, and the thickness of the plastic bags in which the toys are sold. If the toy has a safety label attached to it (figure 83, over the page), then you can assume that it has reached a certain level of safety, but it is the adult's responsibility to make sure that the toy is played with in a safe manner. Remember the law on safety is only improved **after** an accident has occurred, and some articles played with as toys are actually called ''novelties''. Novelties do not have to be as safe as toys.

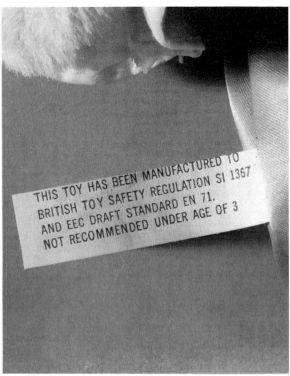

Figure 83 You can find out more about the importance of these regulations from your local reference library.

2 *Will the child be able to play with it?*

What has gone wrong in the situations shown in figure 84?

Figure 84 (part)

Figure 84 (continued)

3 *Can the child try out the toy first?*
There are some toy shops now where children are encouraged to try out a selection of the toys, and you can watch children at friends' houses and at playgroups to see what they enjoy. There are also some toy libraries run by playgroups and organisations like the National Childbirth Trust. What might be the advantages of borrowing rather than buying toys?

4 *Does the toy need any extras to go with it?*
Sometimes it is difficult for children to play with a toy if they have not got at least some of the "extras".

Figure 85 A toy with some of its "extras".

Figure 86

5 *How expensive is this toy?*
You do not need to spend a great deal of money to buy a collection of very good toys such as balloons, a bubble-blowing kit, a bucket and spade, chalks and black paper, a rolling pin and cutters, and a ball.

Why do some adults spend a great deal of money that they cannot always afford on their children's toys (figure 86)?

6 *Is the child interested in the toy?*
The better you know particular children the more likely you are to be able to buy them toys that will please them.

7 *Is it possible to play with the toy in different ways?*
If it is, then the toy is likely to be played with more and over a longer period of time. How would a one-year-old, 3-year-old, and an 8-year-old play differently with the same ball, crayons, or soft toy?

8 *Is this a fashionable toy and therefore likely to become unfashionable soon?*
If a toy goes with a popular television programme what is likely to happen to its owner's interest when the television programme is no longer popular? Fashion is important to both children and adults in many different ways but it is shortlived, so perhaps you would think twice before you spent a great deal of money on a fashionable toy?

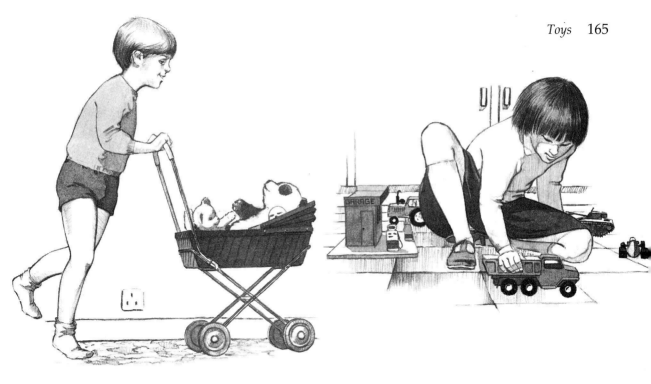

Figure 87

9 Is this toy strong?

It is very upsetting for a child if a toy breaks. Broken toys can also be dangerous.

Did one of your favourite toys ever get broken when you were a child? Can you remember the terrible disappointment?

10 Am I buying this toy because I think it is the right one for a boy?

Do you think that the activities in figure 87 should be positively encouraged?

Toy shops find that construction kits are rarely bought for girls and that toy houses are seldom purchased for boys. Why do you think this is. Do you think it makes sense in today's world? What could be done to make tool kits appeal to girls and toy houses appeal to boys?

Advertisements

It is the job of toy shops, catalogues, and advertisements to try and persuade adults and children to buy more toys.

Look at several advertisements for toys in magazines and on television and ask yourself "Who are they aimed at?", "How are they trying to persuade that person to buy this toy?"

How can children be helped to cope with this persuasion? Should adults always/sometimes/never buy toys they feel children want mainly because they have been well advertised?

Toys at home

It is the adult's task to choose toys carefully, to encourage and help the child to play with them, and then to keep the toys in a good state of repair so that they are safe, appealing, and satisfying to play with.

What sort of organisation and encouragement should adults provide for young children to play with their toys?

How could jigsaws be stored, for instance, so that none of the pieces go missing but so that a young child can get at them easily?

Children do not need to have toys bought for them. They can amuse themselves.

Now try these

How far do you think this is true?

There are several ways to obtain toys economically. You can borrow, buy from, or swop with, other families. You can borrow toys from a toy library. You can buy second-hand toys through newspaper advertisements or through postcard advertisements in shop windows. You can also buy toys from jumble sales and make your own. Choose two of these methods and say what you think is good and bad about each of them.

Why do you think children often like their old toys best and find it very difficult to part with them?

List four objects found in most homes which would make good safe toys. How would you expect a child to play with each?

Name four household objects you would stop a child playing with. Say what is unsafe about each of these objects. How would you store these objects so that a child could not get at them?

Parents can get money to buy new toys by selling old toys. Playgroups often hold second-hand toy sales. The playgroup usually keeps a certain percentage of the money made. Put the following points in order of importance. "If I wanted to sell some of my 4-year-old's toys I would . . ."
check all the pieces were there
wash them
present them attractively.
check they were safe

price them
choose toys my child hardly ever plays with
explain to the child about selling old toys to get money to buy new ones
let the child decide which toys to sell

What safety points would you check when buying a tricycle or a garden slide second-hand?

What makes each of the toys in figure 88 particularly suitable for a child of a certain age?

Try to borrow a variety of toys from a family with young children. Assess each toy according to the ten-point checklist. Do your conclusions agree with what the family have to say about the toys?

Figure 88

It is often possible to make toys which are better than shop-bought ones, particularly if you are making them for a child you know well. Examples of the sort of toys that children like a lot and that it is possible to do very well at home yourself are a shop, a cut-and-stick picture kit, a house-cleaning kit, a tool box, or a personalised cardboard jigsaw. These can be better than bought ones because they can be much more personal, they can be better copies of something that belongs to Mum or Dad, they can be more "real", and they can be more generous in their contents. Make a toy like this yourself. Think about how a child will play with your toy while you are making it.

SEE ALSO

Playing for more about how children use toys.
Health and illness for more about the things children learn to do at certain ages.

See the book *Home and Consumer* (in this series) for more about the advertising and labelling of goods.

If you have a local toy library you might be able to visit one of the sessions or invite a member to come and speak to you. Is there anything you could do in return? Do they need bags made to store the toys in, or perhaps you could offer to wash some of the toys?

Collect, from magazines, several examples of articles which investigate a range of products and compare them with each other, or report on the performance of an object.

This is my own piece of work

At some stage during your course, when your teacher thinks you are ready, you will be asked to do a study and/or an investigation. This will give you a chance to find out more about a part of the subject that particularly interests you. It should also be an example of the very best work you can do.

Do not rush into this, but give yourself time to find a suitable topic. You could try looking in magazines and newspapers to find something relevant and topical.

It often helps to see how other people have tackled a similar difficulty, so look at the articles you collected and in pairs pick out the things which you think are good about each of them. Now put all your ideas together and compile a list of good features an article like this should aim to include.

When you are deciding on the title for your piece of work it is often useful to use a question or to pose yourself a problem and try to solve it. "Why use towelling nappies today?" is better than just "Nappies" because it gives you and your readers much more idea of what the point of doing this piece of work is. "Some women find it very difficult to give up smoking while they are pregnant" is better than "Smoking while you are pregnant" because it describes a very real problem and so is much more interesting.

Try not to choose too big a topic. A small area of work researched in detail is better than rushing through an enormous subject. "How and what do 3-year-olds talk about?" is better than "All about 3-year-olds". It would take a big book to write everything down that is important about 3-year-olds! "What do one-year-old children eat?" is not as interesting as asking "How much salt is there in the food a one-year-old baby might eat in one day?". There are lots of books and leaflets suggesting what to give children to eat, but it would not be nearly so easy to find an answer to the second question, so your work would be original and important to do.

Make sure your study or investigation involves you in doing something other than bookwork. It would be best if you had some contact with families and children. This will make it more interesting for you and will result in your study being much more relevant. There are families and young children everywhere so this should not be too difficult for you to do. You might visit a playgroup, a nursery school, or a clinic, or go to a playground. You could arrange to visit a family with young children or perhaps arrange for them to visit you in school.

Now make a rough plan of the main parts of your project. This will help you to organise your own work load. A good way to do this is with a diagram something like one of the ones in figure 89.

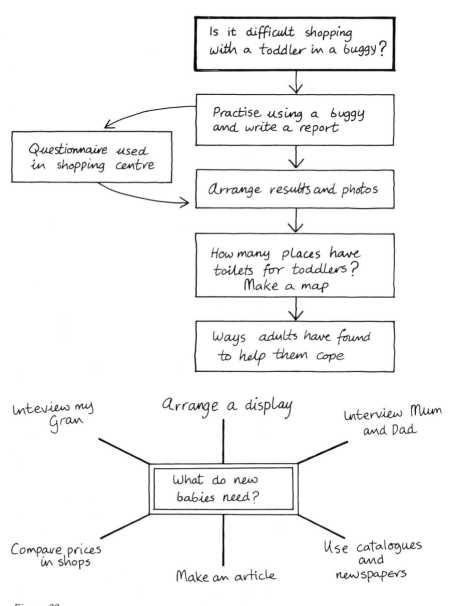

Figure 89

Keep this plan safe, use it while you are doing your project, and when you are pulling your work together at the end include it and show where you went away from this original plan and why. Nothing ever goes entirely to plan and this is okay as long as you can say why you changed course.

To make sure your project is successful ask yourself these sorts of questions at the planning stage: "What special ability, information, or interest can I bring to it?", "Who will find it useful and interesting to read when I have finished it?", "Where am I going to need some help?", "Can I help myself by going to the library, writing to an organisation in plenty of time (enclose a stamped addressed envelope), or by deciding what I need and asking for it clearly and politely?", "Am I going to need any special materials or equipment?", and finally "How am I going to organise my time?". A diary might help you with this last problem.

The way your project looks is important because that will have an effect on the reader. It should be neat and tidy, but also lively and interesting. The use of pictures, photographs, collages, graphs, charts, **relevant** parts of leaflets, and newspaper articles might help you to make your points in a clear and interesting way.

Finally your work should be more than a record of events or a series of pieces of information. Ask yourself "What does all I have found out mean?" or "What are the most important bits in this project and why?" or perhaps "What sort of advice would I now give and why?". This is a very important piece of your work. You should ensure that you have actually done what you set out to do, that you have answered your original question.

When several of you have finished a piece of work like this you could organise a "presentation" where you display your work and perhaps say a few words about it. Encourage each other to ask questions about the work done because this will give all of you practise at putting your main findings into words.

Item for a child

During your course you will also have at least one opportunity to make an item for a child. There will be just as much if not more importance given to your planning and doing as there will be to the finished article. You could make something like a toy, an article to wear, or a meal for a child or you could make something to help the adult in charge of the child such as a recipe book, or a "Good ideas for wet afternoons" book. Be sure to carry out some experimental comparison work on different ideas, materials, designs, and methods, and do not forget to consider how successful you have been at the end. Keep neat but lively records of everything you do. If you can make your item for a real family or child to meet a specific need then you will have no difficulty finding out how far you have succeeded.

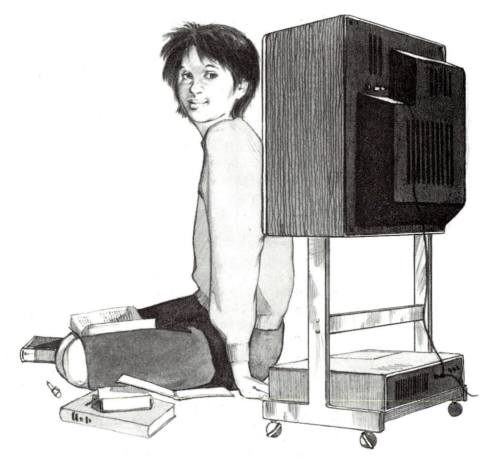

Figure 90 Can you really revise like this?

Is there a written exam?

Towards the end of your course you may sit a written examination. It is important that you know when this is so that you can organise your revision.

If you have missed any parts of the course it is important to find out about these first. This is not revision but it is very important to do so that you give yourself a fair chance of being able to tackle the whole question paper.

It is not easy to revise well. It is much easier to either avoid it or to pretend to yourself and others that you are doing it properly – like the girl in figure 90.

Here are some suggestions to help you to revise well and so do your very best in the written examination.

1) Only do twenty minutes of revision at a time; have a short break and then come back to it.

2) While you are reading about a topic write some questions down about it. After you have shut the book try to write the answers to your questions and then see if you got them right.

3) Our brains find it difficult to remember pages of writing. They remember patterns much more easily. Try to arrange one of your Topics into a series of pictures or shapes with just a few important words. It does not matter how silly it looks!

4) Make a plan for your revision showing what you intend to revise and how much time you will need for each topic.

5) Your classmates are doing the same job as you, so perhaps you could organise the occasional get together to help each other.

Now your course is over

Most pupils in school will be parents one day. Some of you will do jobs which will affect young children directly, and you will all be members of a society that has a duty to care for its young to the best of its ability. The course you have taken will help you cope with this responsibility. It is up to you now to use your skills and knowledge and to increase and improve them.

When do you think the things you have learned on this course will be most useful to you?

When do you think you might need to go and find out more yourself? Suggest several ways in which you could do this. Remember there are three other books in this series which could be of help to you.

Addresses

All the organisations listed below are useful sources of information. I have indicated how they might be able to help you but I suggest that you telephone first to check a specific request. It would also be polite to enclose a suitably sized stamped addressed envelope if you write asking for information.

The Health Education Authority
78 New Oxford Street
London WC1A 1AH
(01-631 0930)

This organisation is part of the National Health Service. It conducts research into health issues, publishes materials, and carries out information campaigns. There are local district health education/promotion units. You can find out the address of your nearest office and obtain a catalogue of the free materials available by writing to the Head Office.

In your local telephone directory you will find the address and phone number of your local **Community Health Council**. They will be able to tell you about local health-related facilities and issues and might be able to provide a speaker to come and discuss a topic such as the provision of health care for pregnant women in your area.

Also in your local telephone directory will be the address and phone number of your **Health and Social Services Department**. They will be able to provide you with details of local and national government provision, particularly financial, for different members of the community.

Your local **Citizens Advice Bureau** will also be in the telephone book. They can give you help with specific enquiries such as how a family might try to cope with debts or housing problems.

Advertising Standards Authority
2–16 Torrington Place
London WC1E 7HN
(01-580 5555)

Ask for information about how advertising is controlled and for details of of the video "Two too many" which looks at the pressure advertising has on children.

The Advisory Unit for Computer-Based Education (AUCBE)
Endymion Road
Hatfield AL10 8AU
(07072–65443)

Write for a catalogue with details of the language processor "Alpha" and the picture-making programme "Hex" which children as young as three years old can master.

Age Concern
Bernard Sunley House
60 Pitcairn Road
Mitcham
Surrey CR4 3LL
(01-640 5431)

Ask for information which will help you to understand more about the needs of the elderly.

Astra Pharmaceuticals Ltd
Home Park Estate
Kings Langley
Hertfordshires WD4 8DH
(092-77 60611)

This company produce a clear leaflet about asthma.

The Beeches School
Beech Avenue
Peterborough PE1 2E8
(0733–43897)

This school has produced a booklet called "Celebrations" which suggests lots of ways of getting involved and learning more about these.

Bio-tex Information Bureau
PO Box 116
High Wycombe
Buckinghamshire HP11 2HS

Their "Washcare Guide" has a useful section on stain removal.

Birthright
27 Sussex Place
Regent's Park
London NW1 4SP
(01-723 9296)

Ask for a list and description of their recent research grants to find out more about how they try to ensure healthier babies and healthier women.

Boots the Chemist Ltd
Nottingham
NG2 3AA

Ask for a copy of their "Babyboots" catalogue.

The British Association for Early Childhood Education
Montgomery Hall
Kennington Oval
London SE11 5SW
(01-250 1768)

This association produces a list of all its publications which deal with topics about children from 0 to 9 years of age.

British Standards Institution
Education Section
2 Park Street
London W1A 2BS
(01-629 9000)

They produce details on how British Standards protect children.

Child Poverty Action Group
1 Macklin St
London WC2
(01-242 9194)

This pressure group produces facts and figures about families and children living in poverty.

Children's Foot Health Register
84–88 Great Eastern Street
London EC2A 3ED
(01-739 2071)

This organisation will provide information about shoe shops which measure children's feet.

Clarks Ltd
14 High Street
Street BA16 0YH
(0458–43131)

They provide colourful, informative leaflets about children's shoes.

Clear
2 Northdown Street
London N1 9BG
(01-278 9686)

For information about an active and successful environmental pollution campaign.

Cystic Fibrosis Research Trust
Alexandra House
5 Blyth Road
Bromley
Kent BR1 3RS
(01-464 7211)

Information about this physical handicap and the research being done on it are available from this organisation.

Department of Transport
2 Marsham Street
London SW1
(01-212 3434)

Ask for their leaflet "Child safety in cars".

Ebury Software
72 Broadwick Street
London W1V 2BP
(01-439 7144)

This company produces a catalogue of computer resources particularly relevant to young children.

ESM
Duke Street
Wisbech
Cambridgeshire PE13 2AE
(0945-63441)

Send for their catalogue which has details of some programmes suitable for use in nursery schools and also information on the "Pop it" keyboard.

Early Learning Centre
Hawksworth
Swindon SN2 1TT
(0793-610171)

This company produces an interesting toy catalogue and leaflets suggesting toys for children of different ages.

Fair Play for Children
137 Homerton High Street
London E9

Ask for details of the work of this campaigning organisation.

Fisher Price
Monk's Mead House
Bath Road
Hare Hatch
Berkshire RG10 9SA
(073-522 4481)

Ask for a catalogue of their toys.

Galt Toys
James Galt and Company Ltd
Brookfield Road
Cheadle
Cheshire SK8 2PN
(061-428 8511)

Ask for a catalogue of their toys.

Gingerbread
35 Wellington Street
London WC2
(01-734 9014)

A self-help group and a pressure group which will provide information about the work it does to support lone parent families.

Handicapped Adventure Playground Association
Fulham Palace
Bishops Avenue
London SW6 6EA
(01-736 4443)

Ask for information about playgrounds for children with special needs.

Help the Aged
Education Department
218 Upper Street
London N1
(01-359 6316)

Ask for information to help you understand the special needs of the elderly.

Johnson and Johnson
Slough
Berkshire SL1 1XR

"It happens to us all" is a lively booklet which clearly explains adolescence.

Letterbox Library
5 Bradbury Street
London N16 8JN
(01-254 1640)

Ask for details of their non-sexist and anti-racist policy towards children's books.

178   *Addresses*

Ministry of Agriculture, Fisheries, and Food
Publications Unit
Lion House
Willowburn Trading Estate
Alnwick
Northumberland NE66 2PF
(0665-602881)

Ask for information about the leaflet and video "Look at the label" and the leaflet "Food additives".

Mothercare
Department YDG
PO Box 145
Watford WD2 5SH

Their catalogue contains information about ways of meeting some of the needs of babies and young children.

The National Association for the Welfare of Children in Hospital
Argyle House
29–31 Euston Road
London NW1 2SD
(01-833 2041)

This organisation tries to improve the provision for children and their families when children go into hospital.

The National Association of Young People in Care
Salem House
28a Manor Row
Bradford BD1 4QV
(0274-728484)

This is a self-help organisation and they will provide a description of their aims.

The National Childbirth Trust
9 Queensborough Terrace
London W2 3TB
(01-221 3833)

This organisation will send you information about the ways in which they try to help families achieve greater enjoyment in childbirth and parenthood.

National Childminding Association
204/206 High Street
Bromley
Kent BR1 1PP
(01-464 6164)

Ask for information about the ways in which this organisation tries to support childminders and improve the service they provide to families.

National Children's Bureau
140 Tabernacle Street
London EC2A 4SD
(01-250 1768)

Ask for a list of their publications and a policy statement.

The National Children's Home
85 Highbury Park
London N5 1VD
(01-226 2033)

Ask for details of their booklet *Children Today*, which contains many statistics you would find interesting and useful.

The National Eczema Society Tavistock House North Tavistock Square London WC1H 9SR (01-388 4097)	This is a self-help group and a charity funding research into eczema.
National Rubella Council 105 Gower Street London WC1 (01-387 8033)	Ask for information about their campaign.
The National Society for the Prevention of Cruelty to Children 67 Saffron Hill London EC1N 8RS (01-242 1626)	Ask for details of the information leaflets this organisation produces and the important work it does with families.
The National Toy Libraries Association 68 Churchway London NW1 1LT (01-387 9592)	This association tries to show that play does matter for the developing child and it produces a journal *Ark*.
Nottingham Educational Supplies Ltd 17 Ludlow Hill Road Melton Road West Bridgford Nottingham NG2 6HD (0602-23451)	Ask for a catalogue of their toys.
Oxfam 274 Banbury Road Oxford OX2 7D2	Ask for details of the work of this organisation.
Physically Handicapped and Able Bodied (PHAB) 42 Devonshire Street London W1N 1LN (01-637 7475)	Ask for information about PHAB clubs.
The Pre-school Playgroups Association 61–63 Kings Cross Road London WC1X 9LL (01-833 0991)	Ask for information about the work of this organisation. They also publish useful information leaflets on subjects such as "parent and toddler clubs" and "playing with junk".
The Royal Association for Disability and Rehabilitation (RADAR) 25 Mortimer Street London W1N 8AB (01-637 5400)	Ask for a copy of the booklet "Abilities and Disabilities".

Royal Society for Mentally Handicapped Children and Adults (MENCAP)
123 Golden Lane
London EC1Y 0RT
(01-253 9433)

This organisation produces a video and a leaflet about mental health called "Let's get it straight".

Save the Children Fund
157 Clapham Road
London SW9
(01-582 1414)

Ask for details of the work this organisation does for children all over the world.

Scholl
182–204 St John Street
London EC1P 1DH
(01-253 2030)

Ask for information about footcare.

Society for the Protection of the Unborn Child
7 Tufton Street
Westminster
London SW1P 3QN
(01-222 5845)

Ask for information about this organisation's work and policy.

Start-Rite Shoes Ltd
Crome Road
Norwich
Norfolk NR3 4ED
(0606-43841)

Ask for information about choosing children's shoes.

The Spastics Society
12 Park Crescent
London W1N 4EQ
(01-636 5020)

This organisation produces information leaflets and a chart called "Benefits for Kids".

Spear's Games
Richard House
Enstone Road
Enfield
Middlesex EN3 7TB
(01-805 4848)

Ask for a catalogue of their products

Tapeworm
32 Kingsway
London SW14 7HS
(01-997 8291)

Ask for a catalogue to find out more about the value of song and story cassettes to young children.

Under Fives Unit
8 Wakley Street
London EC1U 7QE

A national centre for advice, information, and research, funded by the Department of Health and Social Security.

UNICEF
46 Osnaburgh Street
London NW1
(01-388 7487)

Ask for details of their work worldwide.

Index

In this index, page numbers followed by "(A)" refer to activities described under the heading "Now try these"

abortion, 56, 83, 86–7, 88(A)
additives in food, 121, 123
addresses, 174–80
adolescence, 81–2
adoption, 95–6, 98(A)
advertisements for toys, 165
aggressive feelings, 105(A)
allergy, 121
amniocentesis, 55
ante-natal care, 45, 87–8, 88(A), 118
arranged marriages, 97
artificial insemination, 87

babies, 12–18, 18–19(A)
    cost of having, 17
    cost of layette, 52(A)
    image of, 12
    learning to talk, 152–4
    nappies, 16–17
    new born, 13–14
    test-tube, 87
    time to care for, 14–16
baby foods, 117, 120–21
babysitters, 35–7, 39–40(A)
barefoot walking, 112, 113
behaviour, 82–3
    see also under feelings and behaviour
birth certificate, 14, 96
birth weight, 14
birthday parties, 28, 31
books, 20, 22–4, 24–5(A), 129(A)
    home-made, 23, 24(A), 155
    libraries, 22–3, 25(A)
    list of recommended, 25(A)
    nursery rhymes, 155
bottle feeding, 44, 119
boys, treatment and behaviour of, 103–4, 106–7(A), 165
breakfast menus, 123(A)
breast-feeding, 44, 119, 123(A)
buying clothes, 48–9
buying toys, 161–5

calcium, in food, 118
car, travel by, 139
car parking (orange badge scheme), 64(A)
cardboard box toys, 159–60
Carnival, 31
celebrations, 27–31, 32(A), 33
cerebral palsy, 56–7
child abuse, 44, 45–6
child guidance clinics, 74
child survival, 43–4, 122
Child Poverty Action Group, 46(A)
child-care, 14–16, 34–9, 39–41(A)
childless couples, 83

"Childline", 105
childminders, 37–9
children
    caring for disabled, 59–60
    in care, 40
children's clothes, 47–51, 51–3(A)
children's rights, 42–6, 46(A)
children's rooms, 134
Chinese New Year, 30–31
chromosomes, 55, 84
clothes, children's, 47–51, 51–3(A)
cohabiting couples, 91–2
comfortable clothes, 49–50
company childcare provision, 38
computer program, children's, 25(A)
conception, 83
contraception, 84–5, 88(A)
coordination, toys to help, 145
coping with risks, 136
cost
    of children's clothes, 48–9, 52(A)
    of having baby, 17
    of immunisation, 69
    of poor housing, 139(A)
    of toys, 164
crying babies, 14, 152–3
cystic fibrosis, 58

deaf people, 64(A), 65(A)
decision-making, vii, 2–5, 6–11(A), 77(A)
dehydration (babies), 44
dentists, 74
developmental checks, 125–7
    see also growth charts
diarrhoea, 44
dietary fibre, 118
dietitians, 73
disability and handicap, 54–62, 63–5(A)
    causes of, 55–8
    difficulties of disabled people, 58–60
    help for disabled people, 60–61, 64(A)
    meeting disabled people, 54–5
discipline, 104
divorce, 91, 92, 94, 99(A)
doctors
    GPs, 73
    school, 73
dog faeces, health hazard from, 128
doll, home-made, 52(A)
Down's syndrome, 55–6, 63(A)
dressing/undressing, 47–9
dressing up, 51

eating out, 137
eczema, 57–8
education of disabled children, 61

elderly people, care for, 92
environment
  and disability, 57–8
  and health, 128
epilepsy, 61
erections, 81–2
examinations, 172
experts, 72–6, 76–7(A)

facts of life, 78–88, 88(A), 89
  adolescence, 81–2
  conception, 83
  contraception, 84–6, 88(A)
  infertility, 87
  inheritance, 83–4
  miscarriage and abortion, 86–7
  pregnancy, 87–8
  ways of learning, 78–9
fads (food), 120–21
families, 90–97, 97–9(A)
  rules in, 104
fat, in food, 117
fat cells, 123(A)
fathers, 88(A), 119, 132, 141(A)
favourite clothes, 50–51
favourite toys, 160
feelings and behaviour, 100–105, 105–7(A), 108
feet and shoes, 109–13, 113–15(A)
fibre, in food, 118
Fid-Ul-Fitr, 30
fitting shoes, 110–11
folic acid, 118
food and drink, 116–22, 122–3(A), 124
  at birthday party, 31
  in pregnancy, 57, 118
foster families, 39, 40(A)
friendship patterns, 93

gardens, 132–4, 140(A), 141(A)
garment label, 51
general practitioners, 73
German measles, see rubella
"Gingerbread", 95
girls, treatment and behaviour of, 103–4, 106(A), 165
gluten, 121
going out, 137–9
grandparents, 74, 91
growth charts, 44

haemophilia, 58
hair, "health life-line" on, 125, 126
handicap, see under disability and handicap
head lice, 129(A)
health and illness, 125–8, 129–30(A)
health visitors, 73, 129(A)
holiday planning, 11(A)
home, 131–6, 139(A)
home-made baby goods, 17–18
home-made books, 23, 24(A), 155
home-made doll, 52(A)
home-made food for children, 121, 122
home-made toys, 52(A), 159, 168(A)
homosexuality, 83
hospital, children in, 128, 129(A)
housing, 131–2, 139(A)

illegitimate children, 92

illness, see under health and illness
immunisation, 44, 66–9, 69–70(A), 71
infertility, 87
inheritance, 83–4
inherited disabilities, 58
investigation, 169–71
iron, in food, 118
Islamic celebration (Fid-Ul-Fitr), 30
item for a child, 171

Jewish celebration (Passover), 30
job-sharing, 38

kibbutzim, 96–7

labels
  for foods, 117, 123(A)
  for garments, 51
  for toys, 161, 162
layette, cost of, 52(A)
libraries, 22–3, 25(A)
  toy, 61, 163
life expectancy, 122

marriage, 92–4, 96–7, 97(A), 98(A)
  wedding celebrations, 29, 32(A)
marriage guidance counsellors, 74, 99(A)
masturbation, 82
menopause, 82
mental handicap, 55–6, 63(A)
midwives, 13, 73
Minister for Children, 5
miscarriage, 86
mothers, 132, 141(A)
movement classes, 146

nannies, 38
nappies, 16–17, 74
National Association for Young People in Care, 46(A)
New Year, Chinese, 30–31
nurseries, 38
  safety at, 141(A)
nursery classes, 143, 150(A)
nursery rhymes, 155–6, 157(A)
nursery teachers, 74
nurses, 73

obstetricians, 73
one-parent families, 94–5
ophthalmologists, 73
orange badge, 64(A)
opportunity playgroups, 61, 62
orthodontists, 74

paediatricians, 73
paint, 144, 145
PALS (Parents' Listening Service), 106(A)
Pancake Day, 30
parent and toddler club, 142
parenthood, learning, 5
parents
  behaviour to children, 101–2
  child abuse by, 45–6
  fathers' and mothers' roles, 88(A), 119, 132, 141(A)
parents' groups, 74, 105, 106
parties, see birthday parties
Passover, 30
"periods", 82

pets, 128, 132, 140(A)
phenylketonuria, 58
Physically Handicapped and Able-Bodied (PHAB) Club, 65(A)
picnic tea, 123(A)
planning decisions, 7–8(A)
plaque, 116
playgrounds, 138, 149(A), 150(A)
   hazards in, 147–9
playgroups, 142–3, 150(A)
   cookery in, 123(A)
   home-made book on, 24(A)
   leaders, 74
   opportunity, 61, 62
   safety at, 141(A)
playing, 142–9, 149–50(A), 151
   importance of, 146–7
   places for, 142–3; *see also* playgrounds
   see also toys
pollution, 128
polygamy, 96
post-natal health check, 127
potty training, differing views on, 75
poverty
   and child survival, 45
   and health, 127–8
pregnancy
   early signs of, 87
   food in, 118, 123(A)
   health care during, *see* ante-natal care
   protection against disease during, 66, 67, 70(A)
   risks to baby during, 57–8
pre-menstrual tension (PMT), 82
problem pages, 76–7(A)
puns, 157(A)

Ramadan, end of, 30
registration of birth, 14
reinforcement of behaviour, 102–3
revision, 172–3
rights of children, 42–6, 46(A)
risks and dangers
   in home and garden, 134, 135–6, 140(A), 166
   in immunisation, 67
   in playgrounds, 147–9, 150(A)
   in toys, 161, 166(A), 167(A)
rubella, immunisation against, 67, 69, 70(A)

salt, 117
school doctors, 73
school nurses, 73
schools
   home-made book on, 24(A)
   special, 61
   starting, 143
scissors, teaching use of, 10(A)
second-hand shoes, 111
second-hand toys, 166–7(A)
sex, learning about, 78–9
sex drive, 83
sexually transmitted infections, 57, 85–6
shoe shop, 8(A)
shoes, *see under* feet and shoes
shops
   decisions by managers, 8(A)

help for hearing-impaired people, 64(A)
Shrove Tuesday, 30
Sikh celebrations, 30
slippers, 115(A)
smoking
   and babies, 128
   during pregnancy, 57, 58
   survey, 80–81
social workers, 74
sodium chloride, *see* salt
songs, 145
sound toys, 144–5
spastic children, *see* cerebral palsy
special diets, 121
special schools, 61
speech therapy, 155
stain removal, 52(A)
step-families, 91, 99(A)
study topic, 169–71
sugar, 116–17
sugar-free drinks, 10(A)
surrogate mothers, 87

talking, 152–6, 156–7(A), 158
tape recording
   children talking, 157(A)
   children's books, 24(A), 25(A)
teenage marriage, 94
teeth, 116–17
television, 20–21, 24, 24(A), 25(A)
   toys related to, 164
test-tube babies, 87
threadworms, 128
"Togs for Toddlers" competition, 53(A)
toxocariasis, 128
toy libraries, 61, 163
toys, 10(A), 63(A), 159–66, 166–8(A)
   advertising, 165
   buying, 161–5
   for disabled children, 61–2, 62(A)
   good, 160–61
   home-made, 52, 159, 168(A)
   sound, 144–5
   threading and posting, 145
travelling with children, 139
tuck shop 122(A)
Tufty Club, 137

unemployment, 99(A)
United Nations Declaration of Rights of Child, 42–3, 46(A)

vaccination, *see* immunisation
Value Added Tax (on children's footwear), 114(A)
violence on television, 21–2
vitamin D, 118

"Walk for the world", 43
water play, 144, 145, 150(A)
weaning, 120
wedding celebrations, 29, 32(A)
West Indian Carnival, 31
"wet dreams", 82
whooping cough vaccine, 66–7, 68, 69
worms, 128, 129(A)
worries, describing, 10–11(A)
"wrongness", 9–10(A)

ACKNOWLEDGEMENTS

Photograph acknowledgements
We are grateful to the following for permission to reproduce black and white photographs:
Andes Press Agency, page 72; Associated Press, page 22 *below*; BBC Enterprises, page 22 *above right*; British Judo Association, page 112; Clarks Shoes, pages 109, 115; Craven Photographics, (photo: H. M. Beck) pages 7, 64 *above*; Dinosaur Publications Ltd, "I use a wheelchair" by Althea, illustration by Maureen Galvani, page 60; Down's Syndrome Association, page 56 (photo: Penny Millar); Edu-Play Toys, page 62 *below*; Sally & Richard Greenhill, pages 13, 14, 29, 47, 79, 144; *The Guardian*, page 146; Camilla Jessel, pages 57, 62 *above*, 104 *left*; Little Chef, page 137; Longman Photographic Unit, pages 23, 51, 104 *right*, 120, 122, 138 *above* and *below left*, 145, 155, 160, 161, 162, 163; © 1940 Loew's Incorporated Ren. 1967. MGM Inc. All rights reserved, page 22 *above left*; Mothercare, page 167; Oxfam, page 43 (photo: Camilla Garrett-Jones); Photo Co-op, page 28 (photo: Gina Glover); Wimpy International, page 138 *below right*.

Acknowledgements for colour section

1: School library (*Network*, photo Katalin Arkell)
2: Library (*Picturepoint*)
3: Chinese New Year (*Sally & Richard Greenhill*)
4: Child's bedroom (*Longman Photographic Unit*)
5: Child's bedroom (*Longman Photographic Unit*)
6: Child's bedroom (*Longman Photographic Unit*)
7: Child's bedroom (*Longman Photographic Unit*)
8: Child's clothing (*Longman Photographic Unit*)
9: Disabled and able bodied children in joint activity (*Sally & Richard Greenhill*)
10: Disabled and able bodied children in joint activity (*Sally & Richard Greenhill*)
11: West Indians, East London (*Impact*)
12: Woman with baby (*Sally & Richard Greenhill*)
13: Man watching child playing (*Picturepoint*)
14: Young boy with Grandmother (*Sally & Richard Greenhill*)
15: Father and baby feeding the geese (*J. Allan Cash*)
16: Man with baby in arms (*David Richardson*)
17a: Victorian dolls (*Picturepoint*)
17b: Noah's Ark (*Museum of London*)
17c: Jigsaw bird in flight (*Museum of London*)
18a: Doll – Rock and Roses (*Hasbro Inc.*)
18b: Indian doll (*Galt Educational*)
18c: 'The Big Bus Jigsaw' (*Longman Photographic Unit*)
18d: Noah's Ark (*Longman Photographic Unit*)
18e: Rag dolls (*Galt Educational*)
18f: Rag doll (*Galt Educational*)
18g: Doll – Glitter N'Gold Rio (*Hasbro Inc.*)
19: Girl working (*J. Allan Cash*)
20: Boy making sandcastles (*Picturepoint*)
21: Children playing with building bricks (*Longman Photographic Unit*)
22: Children studying nature (*J. Allan Cash*)